ENTERPRISE IN THE NONPROFIT SECTOR

This book originated as a final report on a 1981–82 project by the
Center for Policy Research, supported by a grant from the
Rockefeller Brothers Fund.
Project Director: James C. Crimmins
Project Research and Development: Mary Keil
Project Writers: Ann Derry
                Deborah Hudson

Design: Pritchard & Company
Production Editor: Duke Johns

Library of Congress Catalog Card Number: 83-60521
ISBN 0-941182-03-7

Printed in the United States of America

Partners for Livable Places
1429 21st Street, NW
Washington, D.C. 20036
(202) 887-5990

Price: $7

Partners for Livable Places is a nonprofit national network
of organizations and individuals who share an interest in
promoting communities' economic health through better planning,
management, and design of downtown business districts, cultural
and recreation facilities, parks and open spaces, and historic
resources. To encourage a greater public consciousness of
our physical surroundings and their economic and social
consequences, Partners emphasizes the process of partnership,
the importance of local initiative, and the value of cooperative
learning between public and private sectors.

ENTERPRISE IN THE NONPROFIT SECTOR

James C. Crimmins
and
Mary Keil

Published by

PARTNERS FOR LIVABLE PLACES • WASHINGTON, D.C.
AND THE ROCKEFELLER BROTHERS FUND • NEW YORK

CONTENTS

111637

Foreword

The title of this book, *Enterprise in the Nonprofit Sector,* might shock a few readers. It contains two words that many perceive as being contradictory: "enterprise" and "nonprofit." The object of enterprise, according to most definitions, is to produce income. The objective of a nonprofit organization, according to far too many people, is to avoid making profits.

"Nonprofit" is an unfortunate characterization for organizations that serve critical social, economic, and cultural needs. We live in a profit-making world, where the success of a venture is measured by the amount of income it generates. It is far too easy to dismiss the activities of a "nonprofit" organization as being of secondary value, and to ignore the fact that their benefits are quite tangible, despite the fact that they sometimes cannot be measured in dollars and cents.

Not only does the term "nonprofit" ignore the real and necessary contributions that the nonprofit sector makes, it also allows executives of nonprofit organizations, their trustees, their funders, and their publics to believe that sound, businesslike management practices are not necessary in the nonprofit world.

These inaccurate perceptions—that nonprofit organizations are of secondary importance and that they need not be managed with the same degree of skill as a profit-making concern—have combined to threaten the existence of a large number of useful, effective nonprofit organizations. The demands on philanthropic resources have multiplied as the economy has grown weaker. Cutbacks in government funding have cut deeply into the programs of nonprofit agencies, even when those agencies have managed to survive. Organizations that have not been able to develop new sources of income from enterprise activities and that have failed to develop sound management skills are losing the fight for survival.

At the same time, winning this fight is more important today, perhaps, than it has been for decades. As the federal government cuts back on social, cultural, and other programs, nonprofit community agencies are being asked to pick up the slack. Local governments, trying to meet increased needs with diminishing tax dollars in the wake of the citizen tax rebellion, are turning to nonprofit organizations to deliver public services from health care to park maintenance. And the economic crisis is placing a huge burden on service agencies that are trying to meet the needs of disadvantaged individuals who have been hit so hard by our prolonged recession.

Fortunately, some far-thinking nonprofit leaders are today coming to realize that profit-making enterprise is a legitimate and necessary way of sustaining a nonprofit organization in the exercise of its fundamental service role. The case studies presented here attest to the diversity of innovative approaches that some leaders are taking toward the maintenance and survival of their organizations.

Today's nonprofit leaders owe it to their constituencies to survive and to continue to serve. They cannot continue to rely on charity, and they cannot continue to allow the organizations they lead to be victims of poor management. We must become more businesslike, both in our current practices and in our plans for the future.

Enterprise and an entrepreneurial outlook will not come easily; they require us to develop new skills and new philosophies. This book should help greatly. The successes of the organizations featured here can be replicated in nonprofit agencies nationwide; the problems that some of these groups have encountered will keep others from making similar mistakes. The effort to become more enterprising will be considerable, but the rewards—let's call them profits—will be enormous.

Robert H. McNulty
President
Partners for Livable Places

Preface

We set out to paint a watercolor of enterprise in the nonprofit landscape. It is lucky that we had no more definitive objective in mind, for it is all but impossible to corner conclusive data. A good many institutions merge the results of their enterprise activities with other operations. Some aren't even aware that they have such enterprises, and many have figures that are so kind to enterprise as to be unusable. The accounting in the sector is not standardized, and the figures from like institution to like institution in most instances are not comparable. Finally, nonprofits seem to be buried under questionnaires. It is a labor of love to answer these inquiries, for they do take time to complete. Nonprofits have better things to do.

The good news is that our enterprise reporting efforts met with enthusiastic cooperation, and we were able to learn a great deal. Where we found enterprises performing well, the real story was often in the human factors rather than in the numbers, since it takes individuals—entrepreneurs—to make enterprises succeed. Where we found a level of success, we encountered dedicated people; sometimes just one dedicated person was enough. Thus, when it came time to order our collective impressions, we found discussion rather than numerical analysis most useful, with the numbers used to test and substantiate impressions. We also came to trust our instincts in listening not just to what we were told, but also to what we were not told. We have combined findings and impressions, statistics and anecdotes, in this report.

Our thanks go to the enthusiasm of William M. Dietel of the Rockefeller Brothers Fund and his associates, Benjamin R. Shute, Jr., and Amy Longsworth. We are grateful to the Center for Policy Research for gracefully administering a grant that was atypical—perhaps they all are. Next, we must acknowledge all those men and women in some 300 nonprofit institutions who spent hours with us, answering just one more question. We are grateful to Professor John G. Simon of Yale University and his colleagues for exploring with us at a seminar meeting some of the issues developed in chapters 5 and 6. Thanks to Gibb Taylor, who interned with us between college and a career in banking, and to Robert S. Cox, who interrupted his doctoral studies to design our questionnaire. Our thanks also to Deborah Hudson, Ann Derry, and Rockwell Stensrud, who shaped in words what the reader will enjoy, and to Nicholas Friedman, who typed and retyped each successive draft.

James C. Crimmins
Mary Keil

Introduction

What follows is a close-up view of enterprise in the nonprofit sector. It is an appraisal of the state of the art as of spring 1982—the issues and problems, the successes and failures. It is offered not as an item for study but as a blueprint, a document with which individuals and institutions can build enterprise opportunities.

At the outset, we should define our terms. By enterprise in the nonprofit sector we mean those income-producing activities that are beyond the normal mission of an institution. This definition excludes as enterprise theater admissions and university tuitions, for instance. It does include "profits" generated via ingenuity, much of it consistent with and parallel to the institution's purpose, as well as cost savings accrued through enterprise. By nonprofit we mean those charitable, tax-exempt 501(c)(3) institutions that serve our society's needs. Within this category, for the sake of focus, we purposely excluded health care institutions (largely already incorporated in the profit sector) and religious organizations.

We chose not to use the longer and clumsier term "not-for-profit." It seemed contrary to our purpose of encouraging enterprise. Although we realize that the term "nonprofit" is often used to describe commercial establishments that are in the red and therefore are without profits, this is not the sense in which we use the term.

We have organized our findings into six chapters. Chapter 1, "Overview," is exactly that. Chapter 2 is composed of eleven profiles of enterprise at work. Each focuses on a specific enterprise, making flesh and blood reality out of the process of entrepreneurship. Chapter 3 raises the relevant issues inherent in the sector's enterprise activities and is organized around the viewpoint of the individuals who must confront these issues. Chapter 4, "Organizational Self-Evaluation," outlines further steps for those who are thinking of launching, expanding, or revamping their enterprise activities. Chapter 5 offers specific recommendations for improving the climate for enterprise within individual nonprofits. Chapter 6 presents some new ideas and mechanisms at the level of institutional intervention that we believe will help make enterprise a more significant factor in the sector's health and viability. Finally, the epilogue strikes a short note of caution about making enterprise fashionable. It is not for everyone. The appendix examines the data-gathering techniques and the study methodology.

Our task in conducting this survey was to look at the nonprofit sector with the minds of entrepreneurs, to probe what makes enterprise effective and useful, to seek how and when enterprise can and should occur, and to identify opportunities and pitfalls. We purposely avoided the bigger national institutions—the Metropolitan Museum, Harvard and Yale universities, the Smithsonian Institution, the Sierra Club, the National Geographic Society—all of which have national constituencies and substantial assets. We chose instead to focus on the small-to medium-size institutions outside major metropolitan areas so that our findings would apply to the many rather than the few. We targeted eighteen communities, geographically dispersed, and focused on their nonprofit institutions, which we selected from local and national directories. Foundations, associations, and other nonprofit "watering holes" helped us to find the unusual case, the innovative entrepreneur, the new enterprise activity. We also pursued news stories, rumors, tips, and leads on entrepreneurs, no matter where they resided. After some six months of interviews, we had developed unique and provocative material provided in confidence and reported in a like manner.

Simultaneously, we mailed 1,800 questionnaires and followed up by phone where we had a measure of response. The net result was some 130 completed questionnaires. (We understand why many nonprofits could not take the time to complete the survey and are enormously grateful to those who did.) It took much time and great care to extract the financial data to be found in the appendix. We then compared the results of our small sample to parallel data from larger surveys in each of several nonprofit fields. The general nature of what we found closely corresponds to what was developed in larger surveys. The confidence in our small sample grew. Still, our purpose was not so much to develop definitive statistical portraits as to get an indication of levels of activity, to assess the contributions of enterprise activities, and to measure changes over time. We found that enterprise contributes to the nonprofit sector and has done so for a long time. What has changed recently is the scale and nature of the activities and the numbers of institutions engaged in enterprise.

The results can be found in chapter 1 and the "Study Methodology" section of the appendix.

To readers who prefer to skim through such reports, we suggest you begin with the profiles in chapter 2, the flesh and blood examples. These will introduce you to a world of dedicated people who want to help and are willing to work at helping in a new way, through enterprise. These individuals may not necessarily be the models for what is likely to come, but they will make the data in the other chapters of this report come to life.

chapter 1
OVERVIEW

*enterprise—something undertaken; a project, mission business, etc.,
especially one requiring boldness or perseverance.* [1]

F aced with the prospect of staff layoffs and program reductions, many nonprofit organizations are beginning to look beyond traditional funding sources. Fund-raising drives still flourish, but they have been supplemented by other income-producing sources, such as summer workshops, real estate developments, barter arrangements, cable television programs, and specialized magazines. There is a sense of explosive activity in the sector as more and more nonprofits search for viable alternatives to government and foundation grants, corporate gifts and individual donations, and fees and admissions that have funded their operations for so long.

In this sampling of a small fraction of the 850,000 nonprofits in the United States, we learned how nonprofit organizations are using enterprise to diversify their funding bases, expand their programs, and stay afloat while other sources of support are vanishing. Sixty-nine percent of the organizations we surveyed have given birth to new enterprise within the past twelve years. Sixty percent generate some of their revenues from enterprise activities. Although in 1981 the increase in charitable giving outpaced the inflation rate for the first time in three years (charitable giving rose 12.3 percent, while inflation averaged 8.9 percent), donations from individuals, foundations, and corporations could not make up for recent cuts in government funding at the federal, state, and local levels. These cuts, combined with an increase in the number of nonprofit organizations, means that more groups than ever are competing for a smaller slice of the "giving" pie. As Edward J. Pfister, chairman of the Corporation for Public Broadcasting, puts it, "People used to tell us, 'By God, whatever else you do, don't make money,'. . . . But times have changed."[2]

The purpose of this overview is to provide a historical perspective and place the budget crisis and needs of the moment in perspective. It also gives us an opportunity to report on our interviews with leaders of the institutions that are dealing with enterprise problems and opportunities. Later in this chapter we will discuss what we found to be at the heart of what is possible and what is not: attitude.

---

1. *The New American Webster Handy College Dictionary* (New York: New American Library, 1972), p. 159.

2. Jane Mayer, "Survival Tactics: Cuts in Federal Aid Lead Public TV to Try a Bit of Free Enterprise," *The Wall Street Journal*, March 10, 1982.

NONPROFIT ENTERPRISE:
A CONTRADICTION IN TERMS?

To many, "enterprise in the nonprofit sector" may seem a contradiction in terms. Traditionally, nonprofits in America have helped those who cannot help themselves; contributed to society's cultural, educational, and spiritual development; and campaigned for reform. Their very name—nonprofit—has often set them apart from the rest of enterprising America.

Yet, "a nonprofit organization is, in essence, an organization that is barred from distributing its net earnings, if any, to individuals who exercise control over it, such as members, officers, directors, or trustees. . . . It should be noted that *a nonprofit organization is not barred from earning a profit* [emphasis added]."[3] Whereas enterprise income earned by a for-profit business is distributed to its owners, shareholders, and others, all enterprise income earned by a nonprofit organization is plowed back into the organization. Most nonprofit enterprise supplements monies the organization receives through "giving"—grants, donations, bequests. Our survey results indicate that enterprise rarely comprises the majority of an organization's total income; in fact, only 22 percent of the groups in our sample earned more than 10 percent of their income through enterprise activities.

WHO WE SURVEYED AND WHY

Our study focused primarily on nonprofits that have tax-exempt status under Internal Revenue Code 501(c)(3), a category that automatically qualifies donors for charitable contribution deductions. The organizations we surveyed can be classified loosely as either "arts" or "human services" and include such nonprofits as botanical gardens, family service organizations, opera companies, universities, and rehabilitation centers. Each of the 130 organizations that completed a questionnaire provided information on its program, financial status (including a comparison of revenue sources between fiscal years 1976 and 1981), investments, and fund raising. The questionnaire included a checklist of possible enterprise activities, as well as in-depth questions on the specific enterprises in which the organization was involved. A discussion of the survey's methodology is included in the appendixes.

---

3. Henry B. Hansmann, "The Role of Nonprofit Enterprise," *The Yale Law Journal*, April 1980, p. 838.

Specifically, this report focuses on the following questions:

☐ What types of nonprofits are using enterprise?
☐ What types of enterprise are being developed?
☐ What are the successes and failures?
☐ What trends and patterns are worth noting?
☐ What are some of the most innovative forms of enterprise?
☐ What legal, organizational, managerial, financial, and community issues are involved?
☐ How can a nonprofit evaluate its assets with enterprise in mind?
☐ What recommendations and new ideas have evolved from this?

WHAT THE DATA SHOW

Although our response rate was low, our results closely paralleled comparable data from other sources. To test our conclusions, we gathered information on thirteen of the types of organizations we surveyed, including associations for the blind, child welfare groups, museums, symphonies, theaters, and zoos and aquariums, from a variety of professional organizations around the country. Their data on enterprise income, where available, support our belief that our sample represents a larger universe of nonprofits. Table A-10 in the appendix provides more information.

Whether these organizations were new to the enterprise field or old hands, over 60 percent of the nonprofits in our sample generated some revenues from enterprise activity, and 69 percent of these enterprises have been started since 1970 (see table).

YEARS ENTERPRISES WERE STARTED	Percentage
Years	*of Sample*
Before 1940	9
1940–1949	2
1950–1959	8
1960–1969	12
1970– present	69
	100

During the past five years, over 60 percent of the group with enterprise revenues have experienced an increase in the amount that enterprise contributes to their total income. We found that the organizations whose enterprise revenues have grown experienced more growth in total revenues (over 200 percent) than did the overall sample (139 percent).

We discovered that few generalizations could be made about the types of nonprofit organizations that engage in enterprise activities. Of the 22 percent of the organizations in our sample that generate 10 percent or more of their total revenues from enterprise activities, there is no concentration of size, geographic area, or type (see table).

BUDGET SIZE VS. ENTERPRISE "REVENUES"

1981 Budget Size ($000)	Enterprise Revenues as a Percentage of Total Revenue				
	0	1–1.99	2–4.99	5–9.99	10 or more
0–100	63	6	19	6	6
101–300	48	11	9	7	25
301–600	60	20	—	—	20
601–1,000	38	25	—	25	12
1,001–1,500	63	12	—	—	25
1,501–4,000	12	25	25	13	25
4,001–10,000	44	—	14	14	28
10,001 and above	—	17	51	16	16

We did find that very small organizations, those with annual budgets under $100,000, in general do not rely on enterprise revenues to any significant degree. Very large organizations, those with budgets over $10 million, all engage in some type of enterprise activity. We found that those organizations with the least motivation to pursue profit-making ventures were the so-called "chamber of commerce" groups—that is, medium-size nonprofits, whether museums, historical societies, libraries, or symphonies, that are closely tied to the traditions and values of their communities. These organizations tend to be an essential part of the community identity and seem secure in the knowledge that the community will support and take care of them. They therefore have less incentive to pursue independent enterprise activities.

More than one-third of our sample generates 80 percent or more of their total budgets through *unearned* income (grants, endowment income, etc.), and of this third, 60 percent have *no enterprise revenues* at all. However, of those organizations that receive 25 percent or less of their income from unearned sources, one-half have no enterprise revenues, indicating a high level of fee or admissions income, but no separate enterprise activities (see table).

UNEARNED INCOME VS. ENTERPRISE—TOTAL SAMPLE

UI/TR[a]	Enterprise Revenues as a Percentage of Total Revenue				
	0	1–1.99	2–4.99	5–9.99	10 or more
More than 80%	20	4	4	4	1
61–80%	6	3	5	1	6
41– 60%	6	3	6	3	8
26–40%	—	3	3	2	6
25% or less	3	—	2	—	1
Total	35	13	20	10	22

a. Unearned income as a percentage of total revenue.

A more in-depth detailing of our findings can be found in the "Data Summary" in the appendix of this report.

THE HISTORY OF NONPROFIT ENTERPRISE

Although it grew out of causes and social concerns similar to those that molded the British and European philanthropic traditions, the funding of the American nonprofit sector has always been more complex than its continental counterparts. Professor John G. Simon of Yale University points out,

> Nonprofit organizations in our society undertake missions that are, in other countries, committed to business enterprises or to the state. Here, we importantly, if not exclusively, rely on the third sector to cure us, to entertain us, to teach us, to study us, to preserve our culture, to defend our rights and the balance of nature, and, ultimately, to bury us. And we rely on private philanthropy—third sector financing—to support activities that other nations support with public funds. [4]

Although, for the purposes of this study, we have refined the definition of enterprise to include only ongoing business activities, nonprofits have pursued enterprising ways of earning revenues since the time of the Pilgrims. The first nonprofits developed at the grassroots level, often as offshoots of community or church groups. When such groups discovered that money that couldn't be earned by passing the collection plate could be raised at the church bazaar, nonprofit enterprise was born.

Early nonprofit enterprises developed from the assets and skills that such groups had at their disposal. Volunteers were (and still are) one of the most important assets, and since many were women, much grassroots nonprofit enterprise reflected women's skills and interests: Women's auxiliaries have traditionally held bake sales and rummage sales and sold cookbooks and home crafts to support a variety of charitable and cultural causes. Over time, these enterprises have evolved into solid business ventures, such as thrift shops, bookstores, coffee shops, and gift shops that contribute varying levels of income to nonprofit organizations.

In general, nonprofit enterprises have tended to reflect not only the assets of these organizations, but also the needs of the clients and constituencies they serve. Goodwill Industries' thrift shops developed

---

4. John G. Simon, "Research on Philanthropy" (A talk at the 25th Anniversary Conference of the National Council on Philanthropy, Denver, Colorado, November 8, 1979).

out of the organization's commitment to training the handicapped. Museum restaurants were originally set up as a service to patrons, volunteers, and staff. University bookstores provided an essential commodity for students and faculty. Even the Girl Scouts, whose councils earn approximately 41 percent of their annual income from cookie sales, value the cookie-selling experience for teaching scouts such skills as "learning to work well with others . . . handling money . . . developing the satisfaction of a job well done."[5]

In the beginning, since these enterprises were primarily service oriented, profits often were not emphasized. In fact, whether they made or lost money was sometimes difficult to document, since few nonprofits kept separate books for their program and enterprise activities. There was no need; such enterprises were small and regarded as ancillary to the purpose of most organizations.

"RELATED" AND "UNRELATED" INCOME

According to Susan Rose-Ackerman, associate professor of economics at Yale University, nonprofit enterprise in America developed slowly and without much furor until 1950, when a group of wealthy graduates donated the Mueller Macaroni Company to New York University (NYU) Law School. NYU claimed that since Mueller's profits were going to the university, a nonprofit organization, the profits were exempt from corporate income tax. Mueller's competitor, the Ronzoni Company, sued, arguing that the exemption gave Mueller an unfair competitive advantage in the pasta market. "In response," writes Rose-Ackerman, "Congress amended the income tax code in 1950 to eliminate this exemption. Henceforth, nonprofits would be permitted to retain an exemption only on 'related' business ventures."[6]

The problem of defining "related" has been with the sector since. Both the courts and the IRS have had trouble with the specifics of the definition, which has resulted in a certain nervousness on the part of nonprofits interested in enterprise activities. The university bookstore now has to decide whether selling toothpaste is related or unrelated to the function of the university: Do clean teeth serve the purposes of higher learning? On a more complex level, do such potential nonprofit business ventures as a university's genetic engineering lab or a restaurant run by handicapped workers constitute related or unrelated income?

5. Girl Scouts of America, "Girl Scout Cookie Backgrounder" (New York: Girl Scouts of America, n.d.).

6. Susan Rose-Ackerman, *Unfair Competition and Corporate Income Taxation*, Program on Non-Profit Organizations, Yale University, Working Paper 37, pp. 1–2.

Says Rose-Ackerman: "As non-profits try to enter new fields . . . Congress and the IRS must decide whether to facilitate or impede these activities through the income tax laws."

"THE GREAT SOCIETY"

By the mid-1960s, the entire nonprofit sector was expanding at a prodigious rate. "Much of the growth began with the Great Society programs of the Lyndon Johnson era, which were established in an attempt to help the nation cope with an increasingly complex social and technical society."[7]

One of the most entrepreneurial brainchildren of this period was the Community Development Corporation (CDC) program, designed to encourage small business development in economically disadvantaged areas. CDCs are nonprofit organizations originally supported by federal government funding and set up in low-income communities across the United States. They offer an array of development-oriented programs, which include operating business enterprises; assisting neighborhood entrepreneurs; and building, rehabilitating, and managing housing. Considered by some to be the "granddaddies of nonprofit enterprise," CDCs have stimulated business in many low-income areas, and the positive "fallout" of the CDC movement has filtered into the rest of the nonprofit sector as well. Nonetheless, the longevity of their experience with enterprise also highlights many of the problems and issues that arise. Their failures have been as noteworthy as their successes.

ENTERPRISE PIONEERS

The other important pioneers in the nonprofit enterprise movement were organizations that had difficulty attracting outside funding: Drug and alcohol rehabilitation centers; halfway houses for ex-convicts; and programs for the mentally, physically, or emotionally handicapped have had to turn to self-generated income from the outset. Rather than be subject to the vagaries of governmental or philanthropic support, many of these groups have been able simultaneously to serve the needs of their clientele and to generate necessary income. The key to success is one valuable asset: an available labor pool.

Nonprofits that offer therapeutic and rehabilitative assistance to their clientele have learned to combine such training with enterprise activity.

7. Eugene H. Fram, "Changing Expectations for Third Sector Executives," *Human Resource Management*, Fall 1980, pp. 8–15.

Workers in such programs, called sheltered workshops, carve decorative wooden clocks in Florida; produce pickles, mustard, and ketchup in Rhode Island; raise feeder pigs in upstate New York; and operate a recycling center in Seattle. The type of enterprise developed in such workshops depends on the needs and abilities of the workers, the skills and expertise of staff members or available volunteers, and the needs of the market area.

One sheltered workshop that has managed to become almost totally self-supporting is Bancroft Products in Concord, New Hampshire. A vocational rehabilitation center for the physically, intellectually, and behaviorally handicapped, Bancroft's goal is to teach its clients marketable skills that will help them get jobs outside the organization. The center runs an electronics assembly business, and its long-term contracts with three major electronics companies supply a steady stream of income to the organization. They recently started a firewood business and are considering entering the injection molding field. Chip Rice, the executive vice-president and CEO, emphasizes the usefulness of looking to the for-profit sector for good enterprise examples and says that "Nonprofits must constantly develop new enterprise streams. Managers can't afford to become complacent."

THE 1970s—A TIME OF EXPANSION

By the late 1960s, those nonprofits that had more or less "backed into" enterprise, whether through offering workshops in lighting and set design to support a fledgling theater company or starting a furniture-making business to teach handicapped workers new skills, were beginning to take their businesses a bit more seriously. An air of professionalism crept into the sector, as organizations reexamined their enterprises, systemized their operations, and compared notes with other nonprofits. As nonprofits became aware of the income-producing assets at their disposal, they explored such previously ignored money sources as using facility downtime, licensing the institution's name, and tapping new markets for goods and services. Universities calculated the expense of dormitories and classrooms standing empty all summer and opened their doors for conferences, seminars, and conventions. Zoos studied traffic patterns and erected stands selling everything from hot dogs to balloons to elephant food.

With the increased funding opportunities of "The Great Society," programs began to expand, which led to a need for more income and also to new possibilities for income-generating activities. The entire nonprofit sector was experiencing a scale of enterprise that simply hadn't existed twenty or even ten years before. It was highly visible in the larger institutions, where previously small museum gift shops were growing and making profits on everything from reproductions to stationery to bath towels. The effect filtered down to the small- and medium-size nonprofits; suddenly, everyone wanted to get into the act.

FEDERAL FUNDING: THE $21.2 BILLION CUTBACK

Perhaps not a moment too soon. The rapid expansion of nonprofit programs during the 1960s and 1970s was financed not only by newly formed enterprises, but also, in large part, by the government. "While no one is sure how much federal aid nonprofit groups received, it is clear they shared in the tremendous growth of federal outlays to state and local government, which mushroomed from $10.9 billion in 1965 to $49.8 billion in 1975 and $89.8 billion in 1980."[8] In 1981, however, Ronald Reagan slashed the federal budget, and the bottom fell out of nonprofit funding.

The Urban Institute in Washington, D.C., estimates that federal government budget cuts will cost the nonprofit sector approximately $25.5 billion through 1984. Lester M. Salamon, director of the public management program at the Urban Institute, says that private giving from all sources for nonreligious purposes would have to increase 144 percent over the next five years to make up for government cuts and to keep pace with inflation—a growth rate four times faster than that of the five-year period just ended.

Even though the tax law has been amended, doubling the proportion of tax-free gifts that businesses can make (from 5 to 10 percent of pretax profits), it has at the same time drastically lowered income taxes for many corporations and top-bracket taxpayers. According to Brian O'Connell, president of Independent Sector, a coalition of national voluntary and philanthropic groups, this effectively reduces incentives for large charitable contributions. Other changes in the law, those which allow taxpayers who don't itemize other deductions to deduct charitable contributions, will encourage giving among lower- and middle-income taxpayers but will not make up the loss.

Federal cuts have also put the pinch on state and local governments, thus limiting the "filtering down effect" and curtailing funds available at the local level.

The response to this grim news, for many organizations in the sector, is "to act entrepreneurially. . . . A growing number of charitable organizations . . . have realized that if they're going to make it at all in the 1980s, they're going to make it on their own. . . . Non-profits are

8. Neal R. Peirce and Erin MacLellan, "Nonprofit Groups Are Trying to Learn How to Cope with Federal Budget Cuts," *National Journal*, August 22, 1981.

either selling products closely tied to their charities, or at least implementing sound business techniques in running the organizations."[9]

Organizations with a history of giving-oriented funding are considering enterprise for the first time. They have begun to reevaluate their managerial practices and count their available assets. Gift shops, extra land, and skilled staff members are considered with a newly entrepreneurial eye. Boards members are consulted for their business expertise. Employees are drafted from the for-profit sector. As traditional income sources become scarce, the nonprofit sector has begun to develop an entire spectrum of income-producing possibilities. Scott McBride, president of Marketing General, Inc., a for-profit Washington, D.C., consultant to nonprofits, says, "I don't think the public is ready to see them [nonprofits] putting out automobiles or manufacturing perfume . . . but it's difficult to envision what nonprofits *can't* do [emphasis added]."[10]

THE SPECTRUM OF NONPROFIT ENTERPRISE

Although nonprofit enterprise is as old as the nonprofit sector itself, in our survey we discovered that, until very recently, most nonprofit enterprises were somewhat casual in nature. They often started as services to patrons, clients, or constituencies and were not really expected to contribute substantial income to the organization. Such classic nonprofit businesses as museum gift shops, university bookstores, and junior league cookbooks were often started by volunteer workers and didn't necessarily even turn a profit.

But as additional goods and services became a part of these "casual" enterprises, many organizations began to see that they were sitting on a wealth of income-producing possibilities. The museum gift shop that sold postcards could also sell reproductions, posters, and tote bags. It could branch out into mail order, reaching a much larger clientele. It could sell the use of its name for consumer articles ranging from clothing to coffee pots. It could offer museum tours around the world and from there start a full-scale travel service.

Our survey found that nonprofit enterprise has developed across a wide spectrum, ranging, at the near end, from enterprises *closely related* to the organization's program (ticket sales, tuitions, admissions) to, at the far end, business endeavors basically *unrelated* to the organization's program (real estate development, investments in industry).

9. Dave Lindorff, "Lending a Hand to the Poor," *Venture*, October 1981, pp. 86-92.
10. Dexter C. Hutchins, "The Nonprofit Alternative," *Venture*, April 1980, pp. 34-38.

THE SPECTRUM OF NONPROFIT ENTERPRISE

NEAR/ related to program ·· FAR/from program

| Program | Program Revenues | Convenience | | Selling the Name | | Downtime | Extensions that are | |
		Near	Far	Giving	Royalties		Related	Unrelated
Services specified in the organization's charter	Revenues earned from the program delivery (earned income)	Enterprise activity related to the type of organization closely related	more distantly related	Marketing the name or prestige of the organization to patrons or supporters (quid pro quo giving); contributions oriented	a wider public (licensing the name)	Income derived from the downtime use of an organization's assets	Offshoot of regular program or necessities of the organization	Business venture totally unrelated to any aspect of the program

·· EXAMPLES ··

| Program | Program Revenues | Convenience | | Selling the Name | | Downtime | Extensions that are | |
		Near	Far	Giving	Royalties		Related	Unrelated
Museum: Contemporary art exhibit	Admission charge	Sells postcards/ prints in shop	Cafeteria open to public after hours	Sells tote bag with name/logo of museum	Sells reproductions of pottery in collection	Rents out exhibit halls for parties	Sponsors tour of European museums	Sells air rights to condominium developer
University: Undergraduate and graduate degrees	Tuition	Bookstore; room and board (dorms and cafeterias)	Record department in bookstore	Sells football jerseys, book-covers with name of school	Takes patent on drug developed in laboratory—royalties earned; software developed, sold	Sells computer downtime; corporations use dorms and classrooms for conferences	Athletic department runs summer clinics	Leases extra land to farmers; real estate development
Rehabilitation program: Job training and counseling to handicapped	Fee for services (client pays and/or government reimburses)	Sells special supplies; provides family counseling	Provides taxi service for handicapped—rides for a fee	Sells T-shirts with name of organization	Sells manual explaining how to replicate its program; consulting	Sells counselor downtime to corporations	Sells product produced by handicapped workers	Invests money in solar energy company
Orchestra: Symphonic performances	Ticket sales	Sells programs at performances	Sells drinks during intermission	Sells mugs, paperweights with orchestra name/logo	Produces records of performances; television performances	Rents out hall during downtime	Offers classes or workshops on music; offers music lessons	Runs record store

Based on the data we gathered, we have "filled in" this spectrum with eight different enterprise categories under which, we believe, almost every possible nonprofit enterprise can be placed. The table on the facing page outlines the categories and illustrates them with examples. It should be noted that none of the four examples represents a real institution—it is rare if not impossible to find any nonprofit that engages in all eight types of enterprise; rather, they are composites of organizations contacted during our study.

The table starts at the far left with those enterprises most closely related to the organization's program or purpose and ends on the far right with those most distantly related to the organization's program or purpose. The categories follow:

☐ **Program** describes what the organization actually does; that is, the services specified in the organization's charter. Examples run the gamut of nonprofits, from ballet companies to zoological societies to halfway houses for runaway teenagers.

☐ **Program revenues** are income earned directly from program activities themselves, such as admissions for performances, tuition for classes, fees for services.

☐ **Convenience** is any enterprise activity related to the purpose or character of the organization that runs it.

Near signifies those convenience-oriented enterprises that are more *closely related* to the character of the organization: a university selling books or renting dorm rooms; a museum renting tape recorders and cassettes for exhibit tours.

Far signifies those enterprises that are more *distantly related* to the purpose of the organization: a college bookstore selling toothpaste; a rehabilitation center providing a taxi service for handicapped clients.

☐ **Selling (e.g., licensing) the name** is marketing the name or prestige of the organization in order to realize a profit.

Giving is contributions oriented and concentrates on the patrons or supporters of the organization. Opera lovers buy the company calendar and tote bag; supporters of an ecological nonprofit buy stationery and T-shirts showing the logo of the organization.

Royalties reach a wider public and involve selling the good name or valuable assets of the nonprofit. A museum can sell reproductions of pieces in its collection; a botanical garden can license the use of its name on packets of flower seeds.

☐ **Downtime** represents income derived from the use of a nonprofit's assets when the organization is not using them. These can be physical assets, such as space that can be rented to other groups (concert halls, offices, conference rooms), or they can be human resources, such as skilled personnel that are "hired out" to other organizations or corporations (computer programmers, counselors).

☐ **Extensions that are related** to the organization take the convenience category one step further. This involves expanding an enterprise activity related to the organization beyond its immediate needs and clientele. Examples include a university opening the student laundry to the public or starting a computer software firm and a nature center expanding its hiking tours of the Alps into a travel service.

☐ **Extensions that are unrelated** to the function of the organization conclude the spectrum. These may evolve out of physical assets that the group can leverage into income or may be strictly business investments that have nothing to do with the organization's purpose. Examples include real estate development of unused land; investments in any type of business, ranging from oil wells to pizza parlors.

"DEEP POCKETS"

Although nonprofit organizations have virtually every possible form of income-producing activity at their disposal, our study found that actual participation tends to concentrate in the areas of the enterprise spectrum that are most closely related to nonprofit programs. The categories at the left of the spectrum—"Program Revenues," in both "Near" and "Far Convenience" enterprise—are the most heavily utilized parts of the nonprofit enterprise spectrum. This concentration in certain areas often evolves into what may be called "deep pocket" giving; that is, reaching deeper into the pockets of supporters by offering, in addition to ways of giving, new products and services they can buy.

For example, a supporter of the Dayton Museum of Natural History in Dayton, Ohio, can become a life member, pay an admission fee to the museum (on Sundays), and buy knickknacks at the museum store and jewelry and fossils at its natural history shop. He or she may also support the animal adoption program, paying from $10 to $275 to support one animal in the museum for one year, or the "rent a duck" program, in which a family pays $3.75 to raise a duckling for six weeks before the museum releases it back into the wild. Finally, if the supporter belongs to a local nonprofit group, he or she might arrange for this group to use the museum facilities for some program or event and then give an appropriate donation to the museum.

Most nonprofit enterprises are not businesses per se; they are protected "greenhouse" enterprises that provide a way for an institution to deliver products or services in return for donations. "Why not buy your Christmas cards from the museum?" If the institution's name or reputation was not attached to the tote bag, cookbook, or calendar, it might not sell as well, and certainly not for the same price. Goodwill can be translated into revenues. Real estate transactions can also benefit from the institutional name and presence.

This does not mean that such "greenhouse" enterprises aren't profitable, nor that they cannot grow and expand. But they do tend to be limited to the geographic area where their name elicits a positive, giving response. "Greenhouse" enterprises usually expand beyond their home area only when the institution itself has a larger reputation. Launching into an unknown and broader market can be disastrous, and there is some indication that without external support and/or guidance, such ventures should not be tried.

EASY IN, EASY OUT

Most nonprofit enterprises tend to be street-level, retail businesses, such as gift shops, bookstores, and restaurants. They are extremely attractive to most nonprofits because, in addition to being logical offshoots of their services, they are also often another way nonprofits can encounter their publics. In addition, they are ideally suited to volunteer labor. Most of us have had experience with such operations from the other side of the counter. They are easy businesses to enter.

Unfortunately, they are also easy businesses to get out of. Although some nonprofits have such advantages as free building space or facility downtime, and are often sheltered from having to create and promote traffic (some of it comes naturally with the institution), they still encounter all the problems of other retail businesses. Retail enterprises are labor intensive and demand careful supervision; the profit margins are small and breakage and pilferage costs are high. They require working capital, are difficult to make profitable, and often end up in the red in both the for-profit and nonprofit worlds. Boutiques, bookstores, and bistros top the national bankruptcy lists. In addition, in the nonprofit sector such businesses often begin in an ad hoc fashion as services to patrons and may not be managed carefully enough to generate income for the organization.

KEEPING THE BOOKS

In our discussions with nonprofit entrepreneurs, we discovered that one of the most common problems in nonprofit business (and in much nonprofit enterprise across the spectrum) is a tendency toward a generous approach to cost accounting. Space, cost of capital employed, utilities, promotion, and other normal business expenses are usually not attached to the enterprises involved. The cost of goods sold is often the only cost accounted for. Many nonprofits do not keep separate books for their enterprises and their programs, with the result that it is difficult to know how much (if any) real income the enterprise is contributing to the organization. Costing out *all* expenses is a necessary part of determining what a nonprofit should or should *not* be doing with enterprise.

For example, if a university starts a computer programming service during its downtime, it should cost out such expenses as rent, lights, and heat to determine how much income the business is really producing. It is also important to look carefully at enterprises that are already successful: The university's computer programming business may make $1,500 per week; however, if the university rented out computer time on an hourly basis during off hours, it might make $4,500. Although the university is already operating a successful enterprise, another enterprise might be even *more* successful.

Nonprofits have a tendency to welcome *any* enterprise success and not to think, as do successful for-profit entrepreneurs, that something else might gain the organization more income. Could something else have yielded a greater return on the worry, sweat, and time invested? Recently, however, institutions have begun to reevaluate their enterprises and to apply stricter standards of judgment to their success. The problem is that it is tough to look "found money" in the eye.

ENTREPRENEURIAL MANAGEMENT

Successful enterprises in the nonprofit sector, as in the for-profit sector, depend on the skills of the people who run them. An openness to trying enterprise activities on the part of the board and staff members is essential to the success of any nonprofit business venture. If individuals involved in the organization believe that "making money is not the proper role for a nonprofit institution," then it is extremely difficult to start and carry through any type of income-producing program.

But a positive attitude toward enterprise is not enough to ensure its success. The organization's management must also have the business skills and experience necessary to run a profit-producing venture. Management issues touch almost every aspect of nonprofit enterprise— finance, personnel, and operations, as well as relations with the board, the clientele, and the community. If the organization's management, particularly the executive director, thinks entrepreneurially, the nonprofit is more likely to take advantage of the fullest range of enterprise choices. If not, the institution will probably follow more traditional paths of income generation.

The director of a nonprofit organization is perhaps the single most important influence on whether the institution engages in successful enterprise activities. An entrepreneurially oriented director will encourage new enterprise, reexamine those in which the organization is already engaged, and diversify the organization's funding base in as many ways as possible. He or she will look at what similar organizations have done and will seek help from those involved with the organization, whether staff, clients, patrons, or board members, as well as individuals and institutions in the for-profit sector that can assist the organization in the enterprise areas it is considering.

UTILIZING AN ORGANIZATION'S ASSETS

Successful nonprofit enterprise usually involves working with assets an organization already has at its disposal; the stories of entrepreneurs that have turned such assets into successful nonprofit businesses can be found in chapter 2. But sometimes an institution can "earn" a great deal of income by successfully streamlining its existing operation.

Under the leadership of Crawford Lincoln, president, and L. Charles Kuhn, vice-president for business and finance, Old Sturbridge Village in Massachusetts has maximized the profit-producing potential of the institution's assets by bringing its entire operation to an impressive level of efficiency. The five photography labs that previously served the village have been condensed into one, the bookkeeping system has been computerized, and the purchasing for its retail shops has been centralized. In addition, a hydroelectric plant that will produce power for the site is being built on the property. This efficiency has paid off: In the past five years, the profit on the shops in the village has risen almost sevenfold.

Most nonprofit organizations have business managers whose skills lie in keeping the books and watching the bottom line. But in our interviews with nonprofits around the country, we found that there is a dearth of forward-thinking, entrepreneurial managers in the nonprofit sector. Where they *do* exist, they can be found running the most successful enterprises. Where they are lacking, directors and business managers with little entrepreneurial background, training, or inclination are either struggling to build and develop ventures or are turning their backs on income-producing possibilities available to the institution. In chapter 5, we discuss developing and integrating a position called "director of enterprise" into a nonprofit organization, as well as finding the proper person to fill this role.

BETWEEN THE LINES

The board assumes an active role in the income-producing activities of many nonprofits. Here again, the attitude of board members can have a strong effect on whether a nonprofit gets involved in enterprise activities. If trustees adopt a cautious fiduciary attitude, they will tend to discourage enterprise. Knowing the myriad of possible business pitfalls, they may try to discourage "ill-equipped" and "untrained" institutions from entering the sector. A conservative board that would rather not deal with the concepts of "related" and "unrelated" income, let alone sit down and work out a game plan with the IRS, is unlikely to be interested in pursuing enterprise activities. Directors who are themselves unwilling to take the leap into the sector have been known to present IRS regulations and penalties—with the cooperation of their treasurers—to their boards in order to scare them away from any type of business involvement.

Yet a board whose members are entrepreneurially minded can do much to foster the growth of enterprise in a nonprofit organization. Individual members with strong business experience can expose a nonprofit to a variety of income-producing activities. The board can help guide an executive director with little enterprise experience toward and through ventures most suited to the institution. Trustees can provide much-needed contacts in the for-profit world for possible joint ventures, as well as guidance in such enterprise areas as real estate, downtime, and licensing.

For example, the board of directors for Bancroft Products, the sheltered workshop described earlier, is involved in all stages of the enterprise activities of the organization. Most of the trustees are from the private sector, and they have been instrumental in the successful development and running of Bancroft's electronics and firewood businesses. Now that Bancroft is considering the injection molding business, the board is evaluating the entire project, including the capital investment required. The board is also helping the director with the financial review of the entire organization. In this case, it is clear that the board has a great deal of confidence in the director's ability to manage these enterprises.

A MATTER OF ATTITUDE

Reviewing all of our reporting, we have come away with an understanding that forward-thinking, enterprising individuals are the most important motivators behind successful nonprofit enterprises. If such individuals are respected and supported by their institution, then enterprise works. If not, enterprise is likely to fail. Yet institutions that have entered into enterprise often treat their entrepreneurs as outsiders. The "earners" are separated from the "doers," a split that only works against what both groups are trying to accomplish. This situation can waste a great deal of energy, not to mention money. It is our hope that entrepreneurs will follow the path of fund raisers, who had to work to be accepted as a part of nonprofit organizations. It is the responsibility of both parties—old-line staff and new members—to see to it that enterprise and program staff work together, not at cross purposes, for the good of the entire organization.

The problem is that the sector in general has traditionally attracted people who are more interested in the program aspects of the organization than in the business side. Many people who work in nonprofits, often for less pay than they would make in the for-profit sector, do so because they believe in the mission or function of the organization they serve. They have chosen career paths linked to "service" and "culture" and seem unwilling or unable to mesh such goals with the reality of earning revenues.

Initially, therefore, directors and staff members, as well as trustees and volunteers, may resist any form of enterprise activity, fearing that it will somehow detract from the organization's main purpose. When, however, funds get so short that enterprise is the only alternative to cutting programs, staff, boards, clients, and patrons alike are usually persuaded that enterprise represents a worthy, and sometimes the only, alternative.

THE LAST RESORT

Many of the organizations we surveyed turned to enterprise as a last resort—an approach to take when the funding was cut, the program expanded, the donations dropped. Successful nonprofit enterprises often seem to be those that have either been started under the pressure of need or have resulted from a plethora of assets at the nonprofit's disposal. In a lucky few instances, the two joined together; often, however, enterprise seems to flourish among the asset-lean, grassroots nonprofits struggling to survive, or in the larger, asset-rich organizations that have the leeway to take risks and develop enterprise programs.

Institutions that are less motivated by their circumstances or their communities to venture may see enterprise as incompatible with their purpose. Some know that their potential for enterprise is limited, or that their strengths lie in traditional fund raising or fees. Others are simply reluctant to rearrange their organizations or to upset the status quo. Still others are frightened by what they don't know and would prefer to leave profit-making to the for-profit sector.

But it is here that we would like to sound a cautionary note: Funding cutbacks are making enterprise important to even the comfortable "chamber of commerce" nonprofits, and smaller grassroots groups may see enterprise as the one thing that can save them. But it is not the answer for everyone. No matter how successful enterprise ventures may prove to be in the sector in the years to come, they will not be able to cure all of its financial ills. Some institutions will do spectacularly well—their ventures will flourish, they will branch out into other businesses, they may eventually become entirely self-supporting. Others will be able to keep from going under, or from operating with deficits, but will still rely on more traditional "giving" sources or fees and admissions for the bulk of their income. Still other nonprofits are probably inherently unsuited to any enterprise activity at all, because of the organization's structure, because of the type of work they do, or even because their fund-raising efforts are so successful that no additional funding is necessary. It is important for nonprofits to consider the particulars of their own organization—its strengths and weaknesses; its clientele, program, director, board, staff; and a myriad of other important factors—long before launching into any enterprise.

Too many nonprofits are looking for a formula—a grant request guideline for getting into enterprise. But there is none. Institutional assets and community needs should be combined into a formula that will work for the individual nonprofit. The most useful formula is often one that is compatible with the person in charge of making the enterprise happen. When the question is asked, "What enterprise should we choose?", the answer is simply *the one that works*.

THE BOTTOM LINE

The bottom line is that enterprise *is* making an incremental difference. It is not the magic answer. It works for those who make it work. But it needs help and guidance to be really effective. The rest of this report provides additional ways of looking at what is going on and what can be done.

Enterprise is still emerging, it is an adolescent—at least in the arc of its life cycle. It needs careful understanding so that it is not misread, mismanaged, or undone before it has a chance to reach its potential.

Perhaps the best way to judge the importance of enterprise in the nonprofit sector is by its absence. If it were *not* present, a great many institutions would be gone and others severely crippled. Enterprise is important; it matters and it needs to grow, but under careful conditions and within the proper context. The bottom line is the institution's mission, and enterprise is just another means to that end.

chapter 2
CASE STUDIES

The story of nonprofit enterprise is incomplete without a closer look at some outstanding examples of the businesses and the men and women who plan and manage them. By exploring in detail eleven case studies drawn from the approximately 300 nonprofit institutions we interviewed, we hope to convey a sense of the complexities of management and especially of the ingenuity and drive of these nonprofit entrepreneurs. More than any other single factor, enterprise depends on people.

Each of the following cases points out a valuable lesson in enterprise:

☐ At the Denver Children's Museum, the successful strategy is marketing the product wholesale, not retail.

☐ Housing Opportunities, Inc., uses creative financing and consulting to keep programs independent of government support and control.

☐ At Skidmore College, inventive cost-reduction programs are the key.

☐ Southwest Craft Center has been divided into ten separate branches, each one a distinct profit center.

☐ The Des Moines Ballet Company uses barter to stretch a tight budget.

☐ At Wells College, despite meticulous planning and careful execution, enterprise is a risk that hasn't paid off.

☐ At Pikes Peak Mental Health Center, the staff works *with* the IRS and other government agencies to plan innovative organizational structures.

☐ The Shoreline Association for Retarded and Handicapped successfully balances two needs: earned income, and training and exposure for handicapped clients.

☐ The Guthrie Theatre has established a "director of enterprise."

☐ St. John's College has established a joint venture with careful attention to good community relations.

☐ Disc Village is taking creative advantage of state "use laws" and on-staff talents.

DENVER CHILDREN'S MUSEUM
DENVER, COLORADO

When Richard Steckel walked into the Denver Children's Museum (DCM) on July 1, 1976, his first day as executive director, he knew the organization was in deep financial trouble. The three grants that made up the entire operating budget for the museum had expired that day. No new grants were forthcoming, and there were no plans to raise funds elsewhere. "I knew what I was getting into," Steckel recalls. "The board was totally up front with me about the crisis, and even they weren't sure how long the museum would last. But I liked the challenge of trying to make it work. Trouble-shooting just comes naturally to me."

The museum, modeled on the Children's Museum in Boston, had been organized three years earlier by local parents and educators. It was small and exhibits rarely changed—a poor drawing card for the community. The staff of four operated on a monthly budget of $1,700. According to Steckel, DCM had no local visibility, very few ideas for the future, and, clearly, no money. He set out to change that picture on all three fronts "more or less by the seat of my pants."

Steckel's first move was to cut every expense that wasn't absolutely necessary. Then he studied his assets. "They were meager, to say the least. We had a small gift shop that brought in a modest return, a small membership, and that was it. I realized that if anything were to be done, I'd have to act outrageously just to get attention, to let people know we were alive." His staff worked at increasing membership as one source of income, while Steckel hit the street "hustling, talking, making rash statements about how we'd be self-sufficient in five years, and generally going to investors to get them to donate seed money. It started as simple fund-raising because I knew we had to have something to begin the process."

The process he describes is enterprise: making money in order to operate, and using business techniques to do it. DCM has succeeded well beyond anyone's expectations. In fact, it has become a national model for what a nonprofit organization *can* achieve through innovation, enterprise, and determination.

The museum's current annual budget is $650,000, 95 percent of which is earned income. It serves more than 120,000 visitors annually (up from 20,000 when Steckel arrived) and has carved out a reputation for high-quality traveling exhibits, publications, special events, and marketing expertise. The staff of almost 30 is dedicated to what Lisa Farber Miller, DCM's national marketing director, calls "a strategy of self-sufficiency. . .a timely plan for combining educational money-making projects with traditional fund-raising techniques and of using solid financial management and marketing techniques." That the plan has worked is now obvious. In 1979, DCM won the Business Committee for the Arts national award as the cultural nonprofit that has done the most to "foster interest, involvement, and support by business in the organization's activities." In fall 1983 the museum will move to a new $3 million building that will feature about a dozen "hands-on" exhibits for children.

How was all this accomplished? "There was no set plan at first," Steckel says. "Our plans evolved from our way of thinking about our problem. I wanted to get the museum away from its crisis orientation as quickly as possible. I looked around and saw that, in the nonprofit world, deficits were simply taken for granted; everyone sat there waiting for grants to be approved. There's much waste and impotence in that. I wanted to reject what I call 'the vocabulary of losers' and to stop expecting someone to bail us out magically.

"I started thinking that, in order to grow, we needed venture capital, corporate problem solving, and seed money. I wanted to be able to control our sources of revenue, and you just can't do that when you depend on grants. They're finite and cyclical. My aim was to diversify, to have a balanced stream of earned income that had no strings attached. People often think that I came from the business world; I didn't. Before Denver, I worked in community education programs in northern California. But the point is, I kept running up against the attitude in the nonprofit sector that working with the business community is somehow dirty. I totally reject that. There's no reason in the world that nonprofits shouldn't act entrepreneurially; I think it's an admirable goal."

Today, the Denver Children's Museum is managed like a for-profit business. Lisa Farber Miller says, "We learned to take the pulse of the needs of the corporate community to find out how we could help. We initiated a lot of business practices, such as marketing principles, long-range planning, sophisticated financial management systems, market research, and cost-effective programs. We solicit corporate involvement so we, both the corporation and the museum, gain. We're problem solvers for their marketing needs and for our own. We're not looking for donations, but rather for partners in ventures that deal with learning tools for kids."

DCM has come a long way under Steckel's guidance. "It just seemed like simple common sense that if we came up with enough high-quality products that would reflect well for a corporation, we had the beginning of an answer," he remembers. In October 1976, the museum staged its first exhibit under its new executive director. Steckel secured local donations for a haunted house show, and it made more than $11,000.

"The first attempt worked. We had something to go on and the people around here realized we were still around." A membership drive received a good response. "But most of our time was spent brainstorming marketable ideas. We came up with a book concept called Denver City

Games, and we got a nibble on it from Frontier Airlines. However, they made a counterproposal of having a book on board planes to keep kids occupied." So the staff put together *Frontier's Flying Funbook* and got a fee for services. "They put up the money, we hired the necessary freelance people to produce it, and risked none of our own money."

That experience led to a new way of thinking: "Why make 5,000 phone calls to sell what you have? Why not wholesale your goods to someone by making just one phone call?" *Denver City Games* was subsequently wholesaled successfully to a real estate firm. Another book, *Amaze-ing Denver* was sold to a bank—again, at no risk to the museum. "The trick is preselling everything," Steckel asserts. "We priced our time, talent, all the costs, and sold the books on a cost-plus basis. Each book sold added money to the museum coffers. It takes aggressive marketing, but it works."

Steckel tackled problems on other fronts as well. "We're a small museum, and we have always had traffic problems. Our goal was to get as wide an audience as possible for our exhibits." Miller adds: "A nonprofit has to work with the community. We have an obligation to go to them if they can't or won't come to us. It seems that most museums just want to show impressive admission numbers, but we thought that wasn't the right measure by which to judge. Given gasoline prices and cutbacks in field trips by schools, it was clear what we had to do."

They took the museum out to its audience with traveling exhibitions. The first, "Sensorium," a music/drama/language show, was launched with $10,000 in seed money from five area companies. With the initial funds, contract labor was hired to produce the shows and market research was started. "The companies wanted visibility, which they get with their names on the shows. We learned that shopping malls usually have large promotion budgets. So we lined up malls, restaurants, banks, and shopping centers to show our exhibits. They pay us a fee, and offer the exhibit free to the public. Everybody gets something," says Miller. "Sensorium" has been highly visible and successful, traveling for three years to locations throughout Colorado.

Schools were the next market for exhibitions. The Dayton Hudson Corporation agreed to underwrite "Colors to Go," a show about light and colors that eventually traveled to schools throughout the state. "With school systems you have to do your marketing at least a year in advance," explains Miller, "because that's when principals do their budgets for the next school session. We attended district and regional meetings all over the state, and we had 40 bookings before we even began building the exhibit."

"Colors to Go" has been joined by five other school exhibits, all touring in Colorado. Two more are in the works. "They're wonderful, really," she adds, "and we can keep sending them out because there's always a new crop of students to see them."

"We knew we could produce quality products," Miller continues. "So we started asking ourselves: How can our particular talents be matched with the right corporation? What can we offer? What do they need? What is our joint constituency? I think you have to make assumptions about other people's needs and then follow your hunches. Marketing is a term that has many meanings," she explains. "It can connote positioning, research, or sales. At the museum, marketing is a five-step process: (1) analysis of image, (2) strategic planning, (3) market research, (4) development, and (5) sales. For us, marketing isn't only a management tool or vehicle for earned income; it's also a way of thinking that shapes all museum activities."

In an article entitled "Kicking the Grantsmanship Habit"[1] Miller warns, "It is important that strong management systems and capable staff be in place. Long-range planning with regular evaluation periods, accounting systems, staff contracts, and one or two creative, sales-oriented staff are crucial to the success of this process. In addition, non-profits must learn to give up their survival mentality and aversion to selling and adopt instead more positive and businesslike goals of success, profit, growth, and change."

Steckel believes he and his staff are free to operate innovatively in part because the Denver Children's Museum is not bound by long-established traditions. He has a supportive board, a young and active staff, and a helpful community. "We had to have all that," he says laughing, "or we'd never have made it through the first year. You've got to remember how very 'odd' we are. Here is a nonprofit that is generating more than $600,000 per year in earned income—no city, state, or federal government aid at all." Miller adds, "Corporate executives sometimes don't know what to do with us. There are real barriers when we first sit down to talk. They're listening to me but translating what I'm saying about marketing into what they're used to—giving. We're almost always on the wrong wavelength until I make it clear that I do *not* want a handout; I want to talk business. I want to talk ventures. Then we start all over, from the beginning."

Aside from the traveling exhibits and numerous "activity books," the museum is involved in dozens of other ventures. Among them is *Boing!*, a children's newspaper with a national circulation of one million families. DCM produces the bulk of the national editorial material and generates national advertising sales. Children's museums across the country distribute the paper and produce local editorial material and ad revenue. With a $13,000 loan from the American Humane Association, the museum also produced a book, *Kids and Pets*, and sold it to 9-Lives Cat Food, which is using it as a self-liquidating premium. DCM earns 75¢ on each copy. Other projects, either already complete

---

1. *News Monitor of Philanthropy*, January 1981.

or still on the drawing board, include a series of books about such "help" subjects as safety in the home, environmental issues, calendars for kids, and educational cards and toys. Their next offering is *The Secret Life of Ketchup*—H.J. Heinz Corporation is considering using the book as a premium.

One of the museum's most innovative marketing ideas was developed for its membership drive. To avoid postage costs, Steckel got the huge Safeway grocery chain to print a membership form, plus games and puzzles and information about the museum, on every grocery bag in the area, offering membership at half the going rate. To date, 12 million bags have been printed. Membership is up more than 20 percent, and the cost to the museum has been negligible.

Miller says, "I'm afraid we'll saturate our home market. We need national outlets, partly because our ideas are getting bigger. We're selling more creative services that have a larger constituency. But at the national level, since people have no idea who you are, you have to sell harder. The larger the corporation, the longer they seem to take to make up their mind. We have to plan differently for this phase than we did in the past."

Richard Steckel says he's leaving the Denver Children's Museum when the new building opens in late 1983. "A new building deserves a new person. I've done what I can, and it's time for me to move on. New blood is very good, and the present staff knows what they're doing and why," he reports. Are there any limits on growth in the future? "I think most people here feel that you're more flexible and able to move quickly with a smaller organization. But in terms of services? No. There's no end to ideas and uses for them. That's the exciting part."

When asked about enterprise in the nonprofit sector in general, Steckel uncharacteristically hesitates, and then says, "Our track record is helpful. We're known as doers. But other people forget that just five years ago, we were nothing, nowhere. We used our imagination and creativity and *built* this place. I contend that most other nonprofits could do something of what we've done and benefit from it. I see all this panic out there. Reagan cuts the budget and everybody's scrambling around for an instant solution. But there are no magic answers, no instant success. I don't think enterprise is the panacea, either. It can help, and clearly it's helped us greatly, but it's just one part of the puzzle. Nonprofits should diversify, certainly. But they've just got to start using what they've got and build from there.

"I'm very worried about our cultural groups. If you don't think enterprise and business—it's an attitude I'm talking about—if these thoughts didn't exist before the current panic set in, these places are in real trouble. Enterprise takes *lead time*, time for growth. Those who willy-nilly jump into enterprise might find it disappointing and then get defeatist and go back to relying on grants. That would be too bad. Enterprise would not have gotten a realistic chance."

HOUSING OPPORTUNITIES, INC.
McKEESPORT, PENNSYLVANIA

Enterprise is not an added program or a strategy developed to meet the challenge of federal cuts at Housing Opportunities, Inc. (HOI). Instead, enterprise is the lifeblood of this Pittsburgh-area nonprofit and has been since its founding in 1975. The group, dedicated to revitalizing neighborhoods by renovating older buildings and creating opportunities for lower-income families to own their homes, has received only 25 percent of its revenue from federal, state, or local government sources. James Butler, executive director, started HOI in his dining room after many years' experience in a ministry-related agency as a case worker in blue-collar neighborhoods. His main goal was to help lower-income families gain self-sufficiency through financial education. Looking back to the late 1960s and early 1970s, Butler recalls, "The constant problem was decent housing. You might help people with a dozen small things, but the snag was always how to help them find their own place to live." In 1971, he began spending most of his time studying the housing dilemma for the Pittsburgh area's working class. "The government programs did everything by formula; if someone didn't fit, too bad. People have to be *educated* about how to buy—and keep—a house."

Butler began trying to help families break into the housing market. His preliminary plan, the Earned Home Ownership Program, received funds from the Roman Catholic Church's national funding source, the Campaign for Human Development, the Pittsburgh Foundation, local churches, and single-family-home builder Edward Ryan—totaling $250,000. With that money channeled through the McKeesport Neighborhood Ministry, they made down payments for seven new houses. Butler and a few associates found potential owners and enlisted bank support. Their initial success prompted further efforts, as well as an expansion into the rehabilitation of rundown houses. Butler recalls thinking, "We've got something here. We can help. But we need a better vehicle, committed solely to housing. The neighborhood ministry simply isn't big enough." So Housing Opportunities, Inc., was launched.

"There was a lot of trial and error at first," he says. "What people need is solid counseling, and that's what we have provided from the start. We also supply the means to get a mortgage. We supply the house itself. Most important, we help our clients keep it." HOI has made arrangements with a number of local banks to provide a certain amount of mortgage money to families that go through HOI's program. Normal lending requirements are waived and flexible financing is provided, backed by HOI's own loan fund. HOI works with a family for six to twelve months before the special mortgage financing is arranged. And HOI can boast of a perfect record on its home sales: not one foreclosure in its years of operation, even though all 130 clients were unable to qualify for mortgages, even through FHA, at the time they entered HOI's Earned Home Ownership Program. Butler explains the program's success: "We weed out those who are not committed to homeownership. It's what I said about all those formulas. They work backward! We have scrapped that approach and deal with real-life issues. Every case is individually tailored. We go through every expense a family has—cigarettes, diapers, you name it. If, at the end of the inventory, there is $250 per month for housing, then we arrange a mortgage payment of $250 and not a cent more. This way they can do it. It's realistic and it works."

The heart of HOI's enterprise is its revolving loan fund, which allows for the flexible financing offered to families. Monies in the fund come from private, public, and nonprofit sectors. "This pool of money has been very successful," Butler says. "It has attracted 6.6 times as much investment activity in target areas as it has loaned out. It's all local money. And the loans we made have resulted in nearly $2.5 million in mortgage financing." HOI keeps rolling over the monies in the fund and leveraging additional revenues. "The fund is always in motion. The potential is unlimited, and as the foundation of program funding, it is the source most likely to make HOI self-sufficient."

HOI also functions as the general contractor. The agency buys houses and renovates them or builds from scratch for clients to purchase them. Since 1975, HOI has raised more than $1.5 million from churches, builders, local lenders, and area corporations just to keep HOI going. The general contracting has been slowed due to the economy and does mostly rehab work in declining urban neighborhoods. They buy cheaply and renovate all of the "big ticket items," such as the roof, the boiler, plumbing, and wiring, so the new owner isn't faced with major expenses within the first five years or so. "It's those big things that cause people to default on their mortgages," Butler contends. "They don't have the money to fix the furnace when it goes, so they let the whole thing go."

HOI is also in the consulting business. The group has a contract with the Allegheny County Department of Development to provide various types of housing consulting; this and other government contracts now make up 30 percent of HOI's 1981 budget. The biggest help in fund-raising has been the Pennsylvania Neighborhood Assistance Program (NAP), which encourages corporate philanthropy through tax incentives. For 1980-81, NAP contributions totaled $133,946 to HOI. "Essentially," concludes Butler, "we're into every facet of the housing market." HOI has launched a research and consulting department to serve local builders, bankers, and realtors, as well as social service nonprofits and the government. The organization's newest effort to increase its self-sufficiency is its wholly owned feeder company, Quality Craft, Inc., a for-profit construction company with its own board of directors. Quality Craft will use HOI contacts both to obtain government contracts and to get smaller jobs. Whereas HOI is focused on lower-middle-class communities, Quality Craft will target itself in affluent neighborhoods in order to expand profit opportunities. Butler would especially like to see the company "become involved in forming investor syndicates to finance rehabilitation work." Quality Craft's revenues will flow to HOI.

Housing Opportunities, Inc., gets no tax breaks; according to Butler, "We're just like U.S. Steel; we pay taxes on everything." Real estate taxes are the biggest chunk, and there are no nonprofit rates on those. Since HOI still runs at a deficit, taxes have not yet become a problem. "In this kind of work, there are lots of taxes, all the time," he reports.

Asked about how secure HOI is, Butler responds, "These times are terrible for housing, and in the Greater Pittsburgh area it's more like a depression than a recession. So it's not working as well as I'd like." Asked for his views on enterprise in the social services sector, Butler heats up. "Nonprofits are falling left and right because they've relied on the government for so long. They have got to learn to align themselves within the marketplace, to stand up and see the whole horizon, to use their expertise and build on it. That's what we did at HOI. You can make money selling what you know to someone who needs it. I think you have to think like Procter & Gamble. I mean, look at your service as a product, and then look closely at your market. It's the only way I see to be independent and creative—and to help people. That's what we're here to do, and we have to do it on our own."

SKIDMORE COLLEGE
SARATOGA SPRINGS, NEW YORK

Every nonprofit institution is looking for ways to cut operational costs and to find new sources of income as well. Sometimes "profitable enterprise" takes the form of looking at cost centers that make up "essential services"—light, heat, maintenance—and finding new ways to make them less expensive. This is what happened at Skidmore College in Saratoga Springs, New York, where winters can be long and cold for the 2,130 students and 535 employees.

One day in early 1979, Stephen Harran, Jr., Skidmore's director of business operations and a trained engineer, saw a small article in the *Chronicle of Higher Education* reporting that the University of Rhode Island had experimented with mixing waste automotive oil with #6 residual oil (the most widely used heating oil for buildings) to produce a less expensive fuel for their boilers. This gave Harran the idea that there might be an even better and cheaper way of heating his campus. His hunch was supported by the administration, worked out with other staff members, implemented, and proven successful: Skidmore's Waste

Oil Program saves the college more than $200,000 per year in heating costs, or more than 50 percent off of the price of #6 oil.

Harran's first step was to confer with Robert Jarvis, the plant engineer, to see whether burning 100 percent automotive waste oil was feasible. Then he met with the chairman of the college's chemistry department, Paul Walter, to research potential pollution problems. Jarvis first tried blending different oils, but eventually reached the decision that un-diluted waste oil was the cheapest and cleanest to burn. In addition, Jarvis discussed the project with representatives from the boiler manufacturer, and Harran did the same with the Petroleum Institute and major oil companies to determine whether the oil ingredients would be unacceptable pollutants or damage the boilers.

Within a few weeks, Harran and Jarvis had designed a simple means to use waste auto oil directly in the boilers: a series of electromagnetic filters. Asked if this system could be patented, Harran laughed and said, "No, it's like the paper clip. Too simple." In the summer of 1979, Skidmore experimented with one of its boilers and found conclusively that the waste oil burned cleanly and with greater combustion efficiency than #6 oil. After convincing the New York State Department of Energy Conservation that the new method was safe, the college converted three of its four boilers in December 1979 at a cost of $25,400. Once the waste oil program began, this conversion cost was made up in two and one-half months.

During a year of operation, Skidmore burns about 600,000 gallons of waste oil. At that time, they bought used auto oil for about 20¢ per gallon; #6 oil was going for nearly 60¢ a gallon and has increased in price since then. Another benefit of burning waste oil is removing a pollutant that is damaging to the environment because it is usually dumped in landfills. The college developed an annual oil collection program in the Saratoga area. Fifty percent of the oil comes from one supplier, and the rest comes from another supplier who picks up the used auto oil from more than 50 service stations within a twenty-five-mile radius of the college. To increase community awareness, the college initiated a "send your oil to college" campaign, offering donors gift receipts crediting them 10¢ per gallon for tax purposes. They also created a poster, displayed at service stations, that announces that the station is giving "your oil another chance" by donating it to Skidmore.

At the end of the 1980–81 heating season, the college again saved close to $200,000, and the program's success prompted the school to reduce planned tuition costs by $70 per student. In addition, another enterprise was created. As word of the Skidmore solution spread, inquiries began to flow in. In order to cope, the college established the Waste Oil Conservation Service. Its consultants advise other nonprofits and businesses on how to convert to a waste oil system. The nonprofits are charged a nominal fee, while private companies pay a fee comparable to one-third of the first year's savings. At this point, the service is swamped with a backlog of more than 500 institutions wanting information on Skidmore's waste-oil program. The first year's income topped $70,000 for the school.

Ironically, even with its success, Harran believes that the college's program might be short-lived. The United States generates more than 25 billion gallons of waste oil each year, but there are growing efforts in Washington to find new ways of re-refining it and using it in even more productive ways. Such research will take time. Meanwhile, Skidmore's pioneering enterprise created by staff initiative and followthrough has led to several substantial benefits—cost reductions, environmental protection and conservation, community awareness, and a potentially lucrative consulting service.

SOUTHWEST CRAFT CENTER
SAN ANTONIO, TEXAS

If Darrell Bohlsen works by one credo, it's "cash flow first." When Bohlsen became executive director of Southwest Craft Center in San Antonio in mid-1979, the organization was in debt; no one knew where monies came from or where they were going.

"There was no system, no real accounting at that time. It was crisis management. You can't embark on real enterprise until you know where every dime is going," Bohlsen says. The budget was then under $400,000. Bohlsen and a small group of professionals, including lawyers and accountants, inaugurated a system whereby each area of the center would know exactly where it stood. "Everything is divided into discrete profit centers, and our annual budget now runs at $750,000," he reports.

"Enterprise is first and foremost a way of thinking," he continues. "I saw the situation here and thought, 'I've got to sort out the mess, get everyone responsible for his or her own area, then go for the money ideas.'" With the new accounting system, there are ten separate "branches," each one a profit center. Bohlsen and his board can see in an instant the profile for each branch. With the first agenda finished, Bohlsen has begun to pursue his other ideas.

The Southwest Craft Center comprises several different elements within a four-acre area in a historic section of downtown San Antonio. The center operates the School of Art and Fine Crafts, with an enrollment of about 500 each trimester; the Copper Kitchen restaurant; two galleries that sell contemporary, Southwest, Indian, and Mexican crafts; a parking lot; a new ceramics building, now half completed; and a dinner club that opened in April 1983. It has a full-time staff of twenty-four. "Part of our mission is to restore these old buildings," Bohlsen explains. "It's *how* we're restoring them and what we'll use them for that involves the new enterprise."

With no government grants, no United Way help, and the vast majority of corporate contributions going to endowment or capital funds, Bohlsen had to make the center self-sufficient. "Now 92 percent of our annual operations budget is earned. Membership, the two galleries, the restaurant, and the parking lot all help pay for other programs. I'd like to see that 92 percent grow even higher." It will, if one of Bohlsen's new ventures performs as well as he anticipates. "We had a 130-year-old building to restore. Well, the question was, what should we do with it? We got a few of the board people and other prominent city-father types together, and we decided to make it into a dinner club. We had a couple of meetings, formed a separate entity for the club, and projected that 500 members would be enough. Then we faced the quandary: How do we recruit the members?"

That was in May 1981. What happened was a reaction not unlike a prairie fire. "We did it undercover, secretive, word of mouth," Bohlsen remembers. "One man would mention to a friend that this grand new club was going to open next year, and immediately the response was: 'How do I get in?' By August, they had increased the limit to 600 because of the demand. Now they have a waiting list in the hundreds. And the price of the new Giraud Club? Bohlsen reports: "Depending on the date of application, each member pays a one-time initiation fee of between $2,500 and $3,000, which is tax deductible except for $250. They pay $500 more per year—$250 in fees that are not tax deductible and $250 that goes to the center's endowment fund that are tax deductible. They'll pay for everything else as they use the club."

He sees two important developments that go along with the club. "In the first place, you are extending your franchise, your visibility. We'll get people who may not care about art, but do care about belonging to a private club. Then we can infiltrate them," Bohlsen laughs. "The second point is that each club member becomes a major donor to the craft center, yet you are not beholden to him as you might be in other circumstances. The club is the reward."

Bohlsen hopes to realize initial earnings of $150,000 from the club. Since the center leases the building to the club, a percentage of the club's yearly receipts will flow back to the center. "It should help us a lot," he says.

The two sales galleries, the Ursuline and LaVillita-Galeria, and the parking lot also bring in revenues. Tuition pays only 40 percent of the costs of the School of Art and Fine Crafts, so the rest of the profit centers have to make up the other 60 percent of its yearly budget. "People subconsciously divide areas in their mind," Bohlsen asserts. "This is for profit, this is artistic, this is spiritual, and so on. If we didn't divide up this operation along the same clear lines of responsibility, I think we all might have trouble seeing whether we were hucksters or creative people. When everyone sees where they stand, and knows that the restaurant is different from the school but just as important to the overall operation, then things work more smoothly. What I'm trying to say is that the profit centers that bring in lots of money have no problem 'giving' that money to the school. In fact, it makes them feel pretty good."

In our talk, Bohlsen kept returning to the new accounting procedures and how they made virtually every attempt at enterprise successful. "Let me give you another example. We have a parking lot, almost an acre, and last year it grossed $100,000 for us, but we paid a total of $1,200 in taxes on it. Why? Because we could document every part of use for the IRS. Depreciation, staff use, days of operation, etc. We sat here and watched the money roll in, and because of legitimate accounting procedures, we knew we were fine.

"This IRS bugaboo with nonprofits doesn't make sense. I've been at places where everybody on the board would shut up immediately when the initials IRS were mentioned. You have to make everything work *for* you, and you do that by getting creative accountants and lawyers to help with a system. Then you can be as entrepreneurial as you like. I get tired of people who think you're committing a mortal sin by going after the very money that will save you," Bohlsen says emphatically.

Another aspect of knowing where every dime is concerns the board of trustees. Before, board meetings were wasteful because so much time was spent just trying to identify problem areas. With the "branch" system of monthly accounting, it now takes a matter of minutes to see where troubles may be. "Your trustees are the best resource you have working for you," Bohlsen asserts. "It's a terrible use of their time to have to identify problems. The administration should do that. Now the energy of the trustees can be regeared upward, to the future, where it should be."

Bohlsen's philosophy extends beyond his board. "It's a lot easier to have rapport with people in the world of commerce when you're able to show them a profit-and-loss statement that's fully up to date. This has to do with fund-raising, of course, but particularly when you're spinning off ventures to actually make money. What you find is that the outside funders are more relaxed. They loosen up because you can talk the same language. A corporate guy is more willing to listen, more willing to help, when he sees we know where we are and where we want to go. It's respect, and a rapport that's essential."

DES MOINES BALLET
DES MOINES, IOWA

"Cash isn't the only form of enterprise," says Kay McElrath, general manager of the Des Moines Ballet. "If we didn't rely on a barter system, we wouldn't have the space we've got—and maybe wouldn't even exist as a professional company." McElrath believes that because money doesn't change hands in some of the ballet company's transactions, many personal relationships work more smoothly. "We barter for our basics," she maintains, "and it works well for everyone involved."

Until the late seventies, the Des Moines Ballet Company was a small amateur group, operating out of a few spaces around the city. The decision to enlarge the company, its season, and its out-of-town touring calendar came when McElrath and the artistic director joined the company in 1977. It was at that time that a board member, who is married to a member of the Des Moines Board of Education, suggested that the company take over one of the school system's unused buildings in exchange for maintaining the facility. The local system, saddled with a number of vacant buildings, agreed.

The ballet company took over a three-story elementary school, which provided sufficient space for practice rooms, offices, studio space, and storage for costumes and sets. In return, the ballet company provides a teacher of movement classes for the elementary grades and offers junior and senior high school students the chance to substitute dance classes at the studio for regular physical education classes. The school system gets classes that "would surely have been cut out if done on a cash basis," according to McElrath, and the ballet company has a home.

In the exchange agreement, the school system's only stipulation was that the ballet company could not make a profit from the deal. So more barter relationships were initiated. "We now have the one arrangement with the schools, and three other barter situations," McElrath continues. "On Sundays, a church group uses some of the rooms, and they provide a set amount in cash or services. They almost always do work in lieu of cash. Last year, they replaced the dance floor, part of the roof, and some ancient plumbing. Our maintenance costs are zero, except for raw materials."

In another arrangement, a group of independent visual artists uses one of the rooms not needed by the ballet. Again, they pay no rent but offer a variety of services, including graphic design work, posters, and other print materials needed to support and advertise the ballet. "They couldn't afford commercial space, so this suits them fine," McElrath says. "And we get high-quality design work free."

The third sublease agreement is with two area soccer clubs. "Like many Midwest schools, we have a huge playing field that is of no use to us," she explains. "The soccer clubs trade grounds upkeep for free use. While the kids are playing, their parents are mowing the lawn with machines they bring from home. This service could cost us a lot. Now we don't have to worry about it."

The ballet company's 1981 budget was $246,000, supporting fourteen dancers and about twenty-five performances throughout Iowa. A little more than half their budget is earned from box office receipts; the rest is unearned. "Government cuts haven't affected us at all," McElrath says, "because we're too new and too small to get direct federal aid in the first place. We have a different mentality about government support." The state of Iowa gave the ballet an operational grant of $5,500 last year. "Just to put that into perspective, that was the third largest Iowa state grant made that year to an arts organization," she reports.

"We exist because the company is good and getting better, and because of the barter arrangements," she says. McElrath estimates that the money "saved" or "earned" through these setups is between $20,000 and $25,000 per year. "It's essential enterprise, and all parties benefit. The main thing is that it allows us to survive and have a future."[2]

WELLS COLLEGE
AURORA, NEW YORK

Not every attempt at enterprise is going to be successful. Even with good planning and careful execution, surprises—some of them unpleasant—do occur.

"This one seems to be plain bad luck," says Thomas Gunderson, superintendent of buildings and grounds at Wells College. Located in the Finger Lakes region of upstate New York, Wells is beset by hard winters and, like everyplace else, rising energy costs. But the geological formations around the college seemed to offer a solution to heating the 300,000 square feet of building space. Dotted around the area are numerous natural gas wells that are supplying hundreds of thousands of cubic feet per day.

"One of the college's ex-trustees, who lives nearby and had sunk a very successful gas well on his property, got the ball rolling," Gunderson remembers. "He suggested to the board and the president that this would be a way of substantially reducing our dependence on heating oil." The administration and trustees debated the issue and decided to conduct a survey to see if the Wells land might be suitable. The survey

---

2. In May 1982, after the research for this profile was completed, a vandal broke into the Ballet's building and set fire to the space. Loss to the company's equipment, costumes, and sets was minimal, but the physical damage to the building was substantial enough to require major investment. Neither the school system nor the company felt the investment of those dollars into a building of its age was practical. The company therefore moved into a commercial space that is significantly more costly than the terms of its relationship with the school system. But it remains accurate that, without the use of the school building in its early years, the company would never have achieved the financial position that enables it to support the space it now occupies.

cost about $1,000; in mid-1980 the results came in, and they were positive.

It was necessary to raise funds before the project could begin. Within weeks, the college had solicited donations from trustees and other friends totaling $90,000 to pay for the drilling. In September 1980, the well was begun.

"Drilling for natural gas is just like oil drilling," Gunderson explains. "It's a wildcat operation. Gas might be found in one location and a hundred feet away, nothing. The drilling here took two months, and we did find gas, just as we hoped. But we found something else mixed with the gas—water, way too much of it. We waited until spring to see whether we could find a solution, but by then it was evident we had a bad well."

Tapping a water source is one of the dangers of drilling for natural gas. "Formation water is the serious problem—it's just there, and there's nothing you can do about it. We were hoping what we had was 'frack' water, that is, water used to fracture the earth while drilling." Wells College then spent more money to see if they could solve the problem. At this point, Gunderson says, it looks bad. "There's no way of knowing whether a well will work or not. When you get a disappointing one, you do what you can to fix the problem, and if that doesn't work, you're better off shutting down."

The college gets some gas from the well, but college officials knew from the beginning that it would take four or five wells to meet all the institution's fuel needs. Because of the recent stabilization of fuel oil costs, plans to modify the central heating system to accommodate a large gas flow have been postponed. "The well produces enough to take care of two of our fifteen buildings, and to heat water on a limited basis for two dormitories," says Gunderson. "We're still dependent on #6 heating oil for the bulk of our fuel." Wells also has not had the best luck in the timing of their heating solutions. They converted from coal to oil in the winter of 1972-73, just in time for the OPEC price increases. But an energy conservation program has worked well. "In 1973, we used 500,000 gallons of oil. In 1981, we were down to 184,000 gallons. That has helped greatly."

Will they try to reverse their luck and try drilling another well? "Probably not," Gunderson says. "The college has so many other needs that I don't think we'll raise the money to try this again—at least not right now. It's frustrating because we all know the gas is right underneath us and we could certainly use it. But this just isn't the time."

Wells took the financial risk needed to reap substantial savings for the school. The administration and the board approached the project in a professional and businesslike manner, knowing that there was a measurable chance the outcome would not be favorable. After the disappointing performance, they did what they could to solve the problem and when that failed, decided not to lay out the substantial additional sums necessary to bring the well's output up to a more acceptable level. "We did everything right," Gunderson concludes, "but nature wasn't cooperating this time. This kind of enterprise is always a gamble."

PIKES PEAK MENTAL HEALTH CENTER
COLORADO SPRINGS, COLORADO

"Politics, power, profits, prosperity—that's how things get done," says Chuck Vorwaller, executive director of the Pikes Peak Mental Health Center in Colorado Springs. Those four P's have worked very well: Vorwaller and his board have built a nonprofit conglomerate that is a model for dozens of other social service nonprofits around the country. The center is complicated, with interlocking corporations that offer a variety of services to a community of more than 300,000. Vorwaller credits the center's success in enterprise to a number of elements: careful planning, line-by-line knowledge of state and federal laws, close cooperation with government agencies (including the IRS), good use of existing mechanisms and channels, and, above all, innovation. "I want this to be a charitable nonprofit organization in *purpose*," he asserts, "but a business enterprise in its mode of *operation*."

Vorwaller has succeeded and plans to keep on encouraging growth and helping his community. Because of his experience, Vorwaller is called on to give more than two dozen speeches a year to similar groups. The center hosted four seminars on enterprise in 1981, each drawing between 70 and 100 participants at $295 per person. A guide to identifying enterprise opportunities published by the center sells for $95. Vorwaller's speeches, seminars, and workbook net the center close to $100,000 per year. "I'm very emphatic about the state we're in. This is economic survival for most of us. We have to generate revenues on our own, and I think it's done by structuring your organization to maximize your strengths. What we've done at the Pikes Peak Center can be replicated throughout the social service industry. People just need a model to see how it can be done. They also have to keep asking the questions 'what if,' 'why not,' and 'how come' when obstacles are put in their way."

When Vorwaller arrived at Pikes Peak in 1970, the center had a staff of twenty-four and an annual budget of $250,000. His charge was to build a system that would meet the diverse mental health needs of the community, including drug and alcohol treatment. He determined the center's needs with the help of local industry, the chamber of commerce, and other area mental health groups. "Cooperation is key for nonprofits, but I'm afraid that's not a concept that is very popular with a lot of groups," Vorwaller says. He applied for a $1.2 million grant from the National Institute of Mental Health. It was approved, with commendation, and "then Nixon impounded all those funds. We needed the money to get going, and there it was, sitting in Washington," he remembers. "For the first time ever, the state of Colorado stepped in and gave us the money to make up for what the feds were withholding. We were already working well with the state."

Pikes Peak received two grants in 1973, one from the Law Enforcement Assistance Administration (LEAA) and the other from the National Institute on Alcohol Abuse and Alcoholism (NIAAA). Then things started rolling and the real enterprise began. "I never wanted to be supported by the government. The grants helped us begin using profit-making management strategies. That's what I believe the government law writers intended when they set up the nonprofit guidelines—not to keep us on the dole, but to help us become self-sufficient."

The first order of business was to transform an old manufacturing building that had been purchased by the center for use as both a cash asset and a facility to house client services. "We started with a ten-year mortgage. Then we refinanced it to twenty years and made enough cash to go out and buy a motel to generate enough revenue to carry out a new criminal justice and rehabilitation program funded by LEAA," Vorwaller says. "The program worked very well and we significantly reduced the rate of recidivism to the state penitentiary. Then we transferred the program to county jurisdiction after a pilot period of six years. So we now had a vacant old motel on our hands."

Based on the results of a comprehensive feasibility study, the center's board decided the most profitable alternative was to tear down the motel and build a fast-food restaurant on the site. The center entered into a joint venture with a Wendy's franchise in 1979, and both have realized a healthy profit. The center owns the land, which they lease to the Wendy's franchise. The center also receives a set amount of cash plus a percentage of annual gross revenues. "It's a perfectly legal up-front deal," Vorwaller says. "And it gives us more seed money for other projects."

As service programs expanded, the center bought more real estate—sometimes using all the space, sometimes leasing portions to others. Outside accountants helped the board get its bearings. "We discovered that many IRS codes are written in a way that can *enhance* nonprofit status, not diminish it," Vorwaller asserts. "The government has set up a *structure* for self-survival for nonprofits so we can meet human needs. Look at the breaks you get every April 15 for giving to charities. There are many kinds of nonprofits that can be formed and operate well. After studying the law, we looked at our mission differently. We found how flexible the law could be and a whole new world opened up."

But the center found itself spending far too much time on governmental red tape. "City, state, federal—they all want forms with 10 carbons," Vorwaller says. "The amount of time wasted was monumental." The center also started losing staff to better-paying jobs in the private sector. Up to this point, the center was ruled by a myriad of regulations. "We took a look at our options," Vorwaller explains, "and after lots of talk, decided to set up a number of nonprofit corporations under one umbrella." Thus the Institute for Family and Personal Development was formed, coequal with the newly restructured Mental Health Center. The center is governed by state jurisdiction and must, by law, see and help all who come for assistance. But the institute, also a 501(c)(3), is not governed by state law, and need take only those who can pay the fees. Red tape is cut, and the profits from the institute now flow back to the new parent corporation.

"The institute is a separate entity, but has an interlocking board with the center. It's a nonprofit private organization, and it meets the IRS requirements. The board spent considerable time setting up this system, obtaining consultation from the professionals and the IRS," he says.

With the Wendy's franchise pumping money into the center, there were questions among the board members about how to handle the proceeds. Vorwaller consulted with Denver lawyer Peter Guthrie, who specializes in nonprofit tax law. On his advice, the center set up yet another entity, a 501(c)(2), called Pikes Peak Resource, Inc., which acts as a holding company for the other branches of the organization. One advantage of this move is that there is a limit to liability if any of the 501(c)(3) portions are sued. Titles to all real estate and holdings were transferred to the Resource umbrella, which rents space back to each organization. This minimizes a great deal of risk to all bodies. Consequently, liability insurance premiums have been reduced dramatically. There is no limit to the number of organizations that can be sheltered under the holding company.

"Let's say there are several 501(c)(3)'s under the larger umbrella. If you have sizable government grants for services, you channel those funds into just one of those several organizations," Vorwaller explains. "Paperwork and reporting are substantially cut. I believe that you tell your funding sources exactly what you're doing and why. Bring them in as working partners, involve them. Don't make antagonists out of them. Some of the things we've done at Pikes Peak were so new that we had to lead the government funders through the process. Once they understood, we had an ally."

After a decade under Vorwaller's innovative leadership, the Pikes Peak Mental Health Center had grown to 260 employees (from 24) and had an annual budget close to $5 million (from $250,000). Seeing the amount of money being spent on employee medical benefits sent Vorwaller and his attorneys back to the law books. In the IRS codes, they discovered yet another category, the 501(c)(9), which allows for a self-funded medical/dental insurance program with a "stop loss" clause: If monthly claims exceed a certain predetermined limit, the outside insurance company providing the stop loss coverage steps in to pay the coverage. If the monthly claims are less than the contributions, the excess remains with a trust to accumulate. "It gives us good comprehensive coverage and reduces our risk," Vorwaller says. They created the new corporate entity, known as the Center and Institute Employees Beneficiary Trust, to provide health, medical, and dental benefits and to "promote wellness" among the staff. As a 501(c)(9), the trust has other attractions. Vorwaller believes it will be self-sufficient in five or six years because monies flowing in can be constantly reinvested. Money generated by the investments could be enough to pay for all services— as well as premiums and claims. "This corporate option is available for all 501(c)(3) organizations," Vorwaller adds. "But I don't know of many that are taking advantage of it."

As the diverse branches of Pikes Peak expanded, more space was needed for programs. "We serve some 6,000 enrolled clients, for whom we have primary care, and about 6,000 unenrolled, which is more like outpatient service," he says. They found a small shopping center that had gone into bankruptcy and bought it at a very good price from the Small Business Administration. After remodeling, most of it was turned into a service center for the center's programs. The remaining space is rented to other nonprofits. The rentals pay most of the $68,000 annual mortgage payments on the center; Pikes Peak gets three-quarters of the space almost rent-free.

Another of the center's innovative enterprise ideas is yet another structure right out of the IRS code book. Pikes Peak is considering putting its support services for computer, housekeeping, maintenance, foodservices, management, and clinical records—virtually anything that "supports" the center—into a 501(e)(1a) entity that leases its services back to the other branches of the center. This provision was originally set up to help hospitals run more efficiently, but the center's lawyers, working with the IRS, have determined that it can be applied to a mental health center as well. "You have to test the waters, talk things out, and explain to the government why certain statutes are applicable to your corporation," Vorwaller says. Another option for these activities is to spin off a subsidiary that will take care of these tasks not only for the center but also for area doctors, dentists, and psychiatrists, thus generating a profit.

Creative use of capital assets is another area of potential new revenue. "Pikes Peak owns a computer, cars, and other hardware. These depreciable items can be sold and leased back by the center until the items are fully depreciated, at which time they would be given to the center."

Vorwaller believes his enterprise efforts are a means of promoting his organization's social aims rather than an end in themselves and are thus appropriate activities for a nonprofit organization. "We're within our mission, and we're providing more services. The 'health' of the community can be defined in many ways."

The center is exploring a number of enterprise options for the future. One is a health-food restaurant run jointly with the local School of Culinary Arts; and another is a "wellness" center that deals with diet, exercise, and stress management. "These are logical extensions of what we already do. We see ourselves in the business of 'wellness,' and thus are not limited to operating a traditional mental-health center that provides only psychotherapy. We look for ventures that will support our mission, and we consider these possibilities in an integrated, businesslike way. Enterprise management is looking at the bottom line and helping yourself grow."

SHORELINE ASSOCIATION FOR RETARDED AND HANDICAPPED CITIZENS GUILFORD, CONNECTICUT

"There have been major shifts in thinking over the past few years," reports Edward Goldman, executive director of the Shoreline Association for Retarded and Handicapped Citizens (SARAH) in Guilford, Connecticut. "In the past, mentally retarded people were often automatically institutionalized. That was simply the way treatment or maintenance was carried out. Now we know that is not a productive way to help these people. I think the home situation, where a person who has a disability lives with his own or another caring family, is a more beneficial and normalizing environment.

"It's the same within organizations that serve retarded persons themselves. The old way of thinking meant living almost exclusively on state and federal funds and not trying to raise your own funds. But, you see, doing enterprise and aiding the clients here go hand in hand. In order to provide good, productive work that can be a stepping stone to working in the outside world, we must be offering our clients something more than just stuffing gadgets into boxes." To achieve these goals—more independence for clients and SARAH alike—the organization has launched a number of enterprise activities.

SARAH was formed in 1957 and has grown steadily over the years. In 1981, SARAH had a budget of $1.3 million, about 38 percent of which was earned income from a variety of sources. A full-time staff of 50 and a part-time staff of 25 serve the 30 residential and 110 daily vocational clients.

Ed Goldman continues, "Our responsibility is to make our clients' world more acceptable. We want to provide a work environment that mixes able and disabled people together. It's a matter of getting rid of dead-end imagery."

SARAH's first enterprise was a landscaping business. Supervised clients mowed lawns and did general yard maintenance around Guilford. "There was no clear plan in the beginning," Goldman says. "It just evolved. Our planning is much more careful now." The landscaping business led to gathering and selling firewood and then to other services. SARAH now maintains and operates a nine-hole municipal golf course, runs its own greenhouse, sells seed, offers other gardening services, and manufactures, wholesales, and retails a line of quilted boutique items in its industrial sewing program.

The agency's most ambitious endeavors are the two restaurants it operates. One, the Country Squire in rural Killingworth, is open on a seven-day weekly schedule for both lunch and dinner. The waitresses, busboys, and kitchen help, all retarded and some with Down's Syndrome, completely operate the restaurant during lunchtime, supervised by SARAH personnel. The operation is run by professional restaurateurs. The service during lunch may be a little slower than in a "normal" restaurant, but no one seems to mind. The Country Squire, which seats about 100, is working on a marketing plan to increase patronage because the restaurant is so out of the way. SARAH sees this as a business problem, of course, but in terms of the quality of work experience for the clients, the restaurant is highly successful. During evening dining, the work force is a mix of both able and disabled workers. The Country Squire is not yet commercially successful, but it is targeted to start turning a profit soon.

"The concern for profits and the training of our clients are often the kinds of trade-offs an agency like ours has to make," Goldman reports. "But I see our job as one to make it work as a business as well."

The second facility, the Apple Doll House in Guilford, is similar to the Country Squire in operation, with clients serving as waitresses and in all phases of food preparation. On the premises, SARAH also runs another enterprise called Placemats Plus, a retail store selling high-quality aprons, placemats, napkins, and other assorted items, all of which are made by SARAH clients. The agency has now begun to wholesale these products to other shops, and Goldman says he sees this as a direction to go in the future. "But we don't want to let go of our retail outlet because that's where the clients can meet the public."

Balancing out these two needs—earned income and public exposure for handicapped persons—is the continual challenge for social service agencies such as SARAH. "We're at a crucial turning point right now," says Goldman. "We must make our businesses profitable. We never really had to do that before, but now it's imperative."

Goldman has met some resistance from the staff over planned changes toward more enterprise. "The human services field is full of people with a sort of 1960s mentality of not liking or wanting to deal with business. They don't have the training or the inclination. We've spent a great deal of time doing retraining and changing expectations for our managers. In the past year, we've added business people to the staff so we can see where our money comes from and where it goes. We're initiating a business plan. This is all new. I want to hire an entrepreneur full time who will get us into new businesses that will benefit us and those we serve. I don't have the team I need yet, but I know it's absolutely necessary to have it. This staff is very dedicated to the people here, and they're excellent at what they do. They just don't think in terms of enterprise yet. It's new and a little scary."

In the future Goldman plans to make SARAH a "miniconglomerate, mixing able and disabled people together, creating employment opportunities and job placement services, and mixing for-profit and non-profit operations for optimal service." Goldman also wants to launch new enterprises. A retail bakery and an auto cleaning shop are high on the list. "I'd like to be able to *reduce* our government rates for clients because that would be the clearest sign of enterprise success for us. Lowering fees would help everyone. By using better marketing techniques, a more solid business plan, and a more entrepreneurial outlook, I think we can do it. I'm excited about our direction."

THE GUTHRIE THEATRE
MINNEAPOLIS, MINNESOTA

The Tyrone Guthrie Theatre in Minneapolis is one of the nation's most prestigious regional playhouses. Started in 1963 by the British director Sir Tyrone Guthrie, Guthrie presents eight or nine new full-scale productions each year and tours two plays throughout the Upper Midwest. The Guthrie has never been in desperate financial straits, although it has gone through a few years when operating funds fell low enough to fray some nerves. The National Endowment for the Arts even withheld a grant because it was concerned about the theater's declining artistic standards. The grant has now been reinstated.

After getting through the rock-bottom period, the theater's board of directors set two priorities: launching an endowment drive and setting a policy that at least 70 percent of the budget must come from earned income. And in the last five years, 73 percent of income has been earned, mostly from ticket sales. The endowment drive, begun in 1976, now has some $4.6 million committed. To allow for desired expansion of facilities, the theater is planning another endowment drive, but a date has not yet been set. With a 1981 budget of $5.6 million, 148 full-time staff members, and active local participation, the Guthrie seems secure.

"We're better off, but not secure," says John Slettom, finance and planning director at the Guthrie. "One bad season and you're in deep trouble in this business. Our staff and board are thinking more entrepreneurially now. We have to. We feel that it's time to move into areas that will serve us in the long run, and we're going to have to take risks to see if we can get there."

The theater has already implemented a wide array of what can be described as "standard industry practices," which augment its earned income—a bookstore and card shop (which does less well than expected), backstage tours, a magazine, royalties from productions, workshops, artistic consulting, lectures, and a liquor and soft drink concession that alone nets $60,000 per year. In addition, the Guthrie has taken some unusual enterprising steps.

"I came here to do essentially one thing," says George Spalding, who describes himself as the head of the department of making money, "and that's to create a solid profit center within a nonprofit theater. We have to be more self-sufficient, and my job is to find ways to increase our earned income. We don't have a lot of spare cash to go into enterprise, so we have to move very carefully. That means strong staff and board commitment and very good planning."

"The profit people are coming," Spalding continues. "We're setting up separate profit centers that have to take care of themselves—just like any corporation. Marketing and development are crucial, so we're looking at two different avenues of approach: One is to maximize every physical asset we have, like the stage, and see how we can best use it to make more money to generate cash from within the Guthrie. The second is to go after a pool of money—from a foundation, a corporation, an individual—for investment purposes."

Spalding has the experience—he previously worked with three other well-known nonprofit theaters—and the temperament. "I'll look seriously at anything that fits under our umbrella that will make money for us," he says. "This is the challenge and the fun. It's new territory."

John Slettom adds, "we've gotten much more aggressive about use of the stage's downtime." Last year, the Guthrie earned $192,000 by renting the theater to others. Spalding is trying to fill the theater every night that the company isn't using the main stage. He has booked musical groups, comedians, concerts, anything that is "tasteful." But there's a risk involved, too. With the Guthrie acting as booking agent, if a show does not fill the seats, the theater assumes the financial risk. Because of a commitment to do shows by relatively unknown local groups, the risk increases. Spalding has about five weeks each year to work with plus most "dark" Mondays, but, as he says with a smile, "I wish the theater group would leave me more nights free. Then I could really go to town." Since that probably won't happen, he is looking into booking larger stages in Minneapolis for some concerts. "We'll become independent producers. Why not? We've got the connections and we're gaining the expertise."

Another project in the wings is to open a cabaret theater in town. Spalding sees this as probably an in-house venture starting small with a minimum of capital used to start the enterprise. Spalding sees the possibilities this way: "We're in entertainment. We have one stage here at the Guthrie. I want to use our talent to the fullest, and if I have to find more stages for this talent, then that's what I'll try to do."

Cable television offers new horizons to a theater company with the Guthrie's stature. They have already taped two full productions on the main stage, one of them with RCTV (Rockefeller Center TV, a new cable entertainment network), which paid the Guthrie a fee for the use of its facilities and its acting company. "This is such a new and potentially hot market that we have to go slowly and see the best course for the theater," Spalding insists. "Do we want flat fees, percentages, royalties, or what? It gets very complicated, because we're also bound by Actors' Equity guidelines, and they can sometimes restrict our scope." But the potential of cable transmission is clearly attractive. "If we're smart about it and do our homework, there should be solid, steady income in the future." Spalding is also looking into audio-theatrical recordings, an area he feels should yield more revenue. "I'm looking at every aspect of what a theater does—and can do."

Another of Spalding's projects is a software package to computerize a theater's in-house operations, particularly the box office. He is currently marketing the package, named "Guthrie Management Systems," to other nonprofit and university theaters. "I want to make it so a theater could store a whole season on one disk," says Spalding.

Perhaps the most ambitious enterprise project was undertaken last year by Sheila Livingston, the theater's public relations director, who is responsible for finding housing for visiting artists. The Actors' Equity contract stipulates that a regional playhouse must provide temporary housing at reasonable rates for visiting actors (who pay the rent themselves) not more than a quarter mile from the theater. Guthrie has always had to scramble to come up with suitable apartments for its numerous out-of-town artists. Livingston solved the problem and got the theater into a solid enterprise activity: real estate. She found a 100-unit building a few blocks from the theater and arranged to buy it at a very reasonable price. The Guthrie keeps 30 apartments for its own needs and rents 70 to other tenants. In the first year, rentals netted $70,000. "This was initiated by the staff, and the board was also very involved," comments Slettom. "We filled a need that had been frustrating us for years, and we filled it in a solid way. We have the option to keep renting the apartments, or to co-op the building in future years if that seems more lucrative." And the IRS? "We have a good case here for related business income because of the Equity contract. This is a case of actually being forced into enterprise."

ST. JOHN'S COLLEGE
SANTE FE, NEW MEXICO

Hundreds of nonprofit institutions have been fortunate enough to receive bequests of real estate that could be developed in many ways, depending on the location and type of gift, as well as restrictions connected with it. The challenge is to maximize the potential of the asset so that the organization will reap benefits for years to come. This complex and difficult task has many inherent pitfalls. Those real estate ventures that are successful, although very different in type or size, tend to resemble one another in crucial ways: a committed staff, an involved board of directors, a good marketing study, the use of professionals, good community relations, and sound financial approaches.

St. John's College in Santa Fe, New Mexico, was approached in mid-1979 by a local realtor wanting to put a road through part of the 287 contiguous acres around the campus in the foothills of the Sangre de Cristo Mountains. After some deliberation, the college's full board decided to refuse the offer because "we lacked a sound basis on which to decide whether this road would be advantageous or disadvantageous to the college and its neighbors," according to J. Burchenal Ault, provost of St. John's. The offer did spur the administration to decide what should be done with the land. As Mr. Ault reports, "The college got into the real estate development business 'on purpose' but 'sideways.' "

The first step was the formation of a committee to "study, with professional help as seemed necessary, how the college might develop a master plan for the use of the entirety of its Santa Fe property, including, if that seemed desirable, consideration of sale or lease of some of its property in order to augment the college's endowed funds."

In August 1979, the committee began screening possible planning consultants. "At the same time, various local board members, alumni, and friends of the college were asked to join a new committee, consisting of members of both board and faculty development committees and others," writes Mr. Ault. This second committee then chose a firm to complete the first stage of the planning study, a land inventory. The planning firm's costs were not to exceed $17,000.

While these steps were being put into motion, the college applied for a grant of $30,000 from the Independent College Funds of America for the express purpose of helping them decide whether to develop unused property in order to aid their endowment. In December 1979, St. John's was awarded the grant. The college was to receive the services of a planning lawyer and an architect/planner from a New York City firm, New Sources of Funding, Inc.

After the land inventory was completed in April 1980, all parties sat down to thrash out strategy. The inventory suggested two excellent sites for the development of residential condominiums on the St. John's property. The consensus was to "join hands with a carefully selected developer who, with a team composed of an architect, planner, builder, and traffic engineer, among others, could direct and fund their combined efforts to design an optimal development plan—taking into account the college's financial, recreational, and aesthetic requirements; the interests of the neighbors and of citizens of Sante Fe; and the ecology of the land itself," reports Ault.

More committee meetings were held over that summer. The New Sources people advised the college to interview developers and architects to see what kind of deal they would be offered. In particular, the college wanted to secure a good amount of cash in advance to add to the endowment fund. Finally, after numerous meetings, the committee chose the plan offered by William Zeckendorf, Jr., of New York, in association with Nat Owings, senior design advisor and one of the cofounders of the architecture firm of Skidmore, Owings and Merrill. They proposed two condominium sites (totaling 112 houses), a plan which would then leave the majority of the land forever open.

Next, the college turned its forces to enlisting the support of its students and teachers, as well as the Santa Fe community. The board of trustees had been actively involved in all previous development, and its members felt it was especially important to keep the town informed about the college's plans. They approached the Santa Fe authorities twice: first to explain the general idea and later to present detailed plans. They also held "seminars and all-college meetings where students and faculty were given the opportunity to express their concerns about the project," according to an article in the *Santa Fe Reporter*.

In June 1981, the planning committee met with a group of citizens. The condominium plan met with minimal local disapproval. Ian Cook, a member of the planning committee, reported to Debra Voisin of the *Albuquerque Journal*, "We haven't sensed any violent opposition. The sense I get is that people understand the college's position, and if the development project is going to help the college, then, yes, I think there's general support."

Ault's attitude about community criticism is that it was to be expected, but how the college replied was the crucial test. It is always best, he says, to offer "a firm determination to listen, to be willing to be flexible, to accept criticism, to be open and friendly, and to be always available."

In July 1981, the board of trustees accepted Zeckendorf's offer. Zeckendorf will pay St. John's at least $2.8 million for the land during the building phase, retaining the right to use the leasehold and rent the land to the condominium owners under a ninety-nine-year lease. The college will collect rentals for the first five years at $100,000 per year; $134,000 per year for the next ten years; $268,000 per year for the following ten years. Thereafter rentals will be indexed to the prevailing rate of commercially available mortgages and the newly appraised value of the land. With a present annual budget of $4.2 million for the Santa Fe campus, the investment income earned with the $3 million for land plus rental income will go a long way toward easing the annual deficit the college has been making up through strenuous fund-raising efforts.

After city council approval in December 1981 and other reviews, construction is about to begin. The new condominium owners will pay on average about $300,000 per unit, but their privacy and scenery are ensured: The college has an agreement with the owners that there will be no new building on the remaining vacant acreage. St. John's benefits because the venture provides a good steady return, yet does not expose the college to unnecessary risks. Zeckendorf takes most of the risks, but also stands to make a healthy return when the buildings sell.

Finally, the development involves an ethical issue. One concerned Santa Fe citizen opposed to the development said at a meeting that he thought that land given to the college had to be used only for academic purposes. He was answered by Mrs. John Meem, whose family gave the great majority of the land being used for condominiums to the college. "I don't think we ever thought this type of boom would occur," she said. "We naturally would like to see the land remain free of development, but the college needs the money. And I'm hoping it'll be such a beautiful development that we'll show others what can be done."

DISC VILLAGE
WOODVILLE, FLORIDA

Disc Village, a drug and alcohol rehabilitation center in Woodville, Florida, just outside Tallahassee, opened its doors in 1973. Disc Village offers counseling and vocational training programs for its forty or so clients who live full time at the eight-acre facility, and who range in age from about fourteen to twenty-one years old. Unlike most rehabilitation centers, Disc is "doing everything possible to put an end to government financing of the programs," according to Tom Olk, the director. "It takes tenacity, hustle, cajoling, working the angles to stand on your own two feet. We're looking for total self-sufficiency here, and I think it's right that we do. We're trying to help the people we serve regain their own self-esteem, their own sense of worth. As an organization, we have to think the same way, and to me that means generating your own resources in a variety of ways."

The village started out with federal government monies. "That was the heyday for this kind of program," Olk says. "But I realized that that money would dry up sometime soon, so the first thing to do was start planning options. There's something very satisfying about using your ingenuity and creativity in order to survive." Disc Village's budget is still based on "slot allocations," with the government picking up a percentage of each resident's costs, and the center supplying the rest. Olk says their budget is around $500,000 per year now, with enterprise making up "about one-third of our annual income."

Disc Village helps itself in numerous ways. The residents keep their own large garden, raise farm animals, and are trained in kitchen management, industrial arts, and secretarial and bookkeeping skills. "We're doing two things here," Olk says. "Trying to help each person find a concrete skill that will help them when they leave us, and at the same time use each enterprise to help us generate more capital." Some of the cottage industries Disc has previously been involved in include woodcutting, commercial fishing, and a greenhouse.

Their most recent venture is an optical laboratory, set up on the grounds, which has begun turning out prescription eyeglasses and safety goggles for industry. Supervised by a licensed optician who draws a salary, the lab work is done by anywhere from four to eight residents. Olk received a $10,000 grant from the state of Florida to purchase equipment, and then looked for customers. He approached state officials first, and got a contract to supply glasses for a community-run children's clinic. "As a sheltered workshop, we can sell to the state. They save money this way because we can produce at a competitive price," Olk says. "It's a matter of utilizing the state's 'use laws.' "

Use laws are relatively complicated. They differ from state to state, and not all states have written laws. Essentially, these laws aid qualifying rehabilitation programs in social service agencies by providing state funds for clients' (those receiving treatment) wages or stipends. The laws do not guarantee that the state will buy the products that result from the programs. Furthermore, while the laws stipulate that state monies cannot flow directly to the agency itself, the agency still benefits in several ways. Use laws funds go to the clients, but they in turn pay the agency on a sliding scale for rehabilitative services rendered. This fee can be a source of extra income to the agency because the payment is often higher than the related costs. Another advantage is that the use laws enable the agency to make contacts with state department officials, which may make it easier for the agency to sell its sheltered workshop products. Olk emphasizes that this is not an adherence to a "welfare mentality," because clients must assume responsibility for their rehabilitation; fees for this purpose provide revenues by way of the optical lab or any of the other enterprises at Disc Village. Clients in turn learn financial responsibility and a marketable vocational skill.

The state of Florida runs six large hospitals, and virtually every community has a children's medical service, so Olk sees his market for lenses expanding rapidly. "You do some politicking, persuading, explaining, and that gives us the opportunity to grow," he says. "I want to see us at the point where we're supplying most of the state's demand

for eyeglasses. We've also been talking to the military and local Lion's Clubs about doing work for them. The market is unlimited. You just have to go out and talk and sell."

The Disc Village optical lab now turns out about 60 pairs of glasses per day, according to Olk. The profits get rolled back into buying more equipment and funding other entrepreneurial ventures.

Disc is also entering the printing business and has found three local printers who are helping to train the residents. What about infringing on the private sector's turf? "There's no fear of competition here," Olk insists. "The printers welcome our program and donate time to help set up the system. There's enough work for everyone and a great need for entry-level people." The printing operation would be set up much like the optical laboratory, whereby Disc Village provides printing services to other private nonprofit and public agencies. In addition, Disc will be able to handle the overflow business of the printing industry in Tallahassee, which is dominated by the state government and three colleges. "The state is definitely behind our activities, and they don't penalize us for trying to take care of ourselves. They encourage it. We have a proven track record of success, and I think it's because we try to do it right from the beginning. We attempt not to entangle ourselves with the bureaucracy as much as possible, and we try to stay away from all the strings that get attached when you're dependent on government grants."

Like other nonprofit administrators who have gotten into enterprise activities, Olk believes success is a matter of attitude. "The specific venture itself is almost secondary—and it can be almost anything under the sun that will produce revenue," he says. "The main point is using your resources and having the conviction to do things the best way. I want to take one dollar and turn it into three. Now, what's the best way to do that? Once you start thinking, you'd be surprised at how many options there are.

"What we're doing is just the tip of the proverbial iceberg. Our operation can and should be replicated all over the country. There's no reason other nonprofits shouldn't be utilizing use laws and other programs out there. It takes money to be humanitarian, and that's our basic goal. I'm afraid most human-service bureaucracies haven't gotten the message yet." Olk is trying to spread the word as far as possible about Disc Village and its operations. "It pains me to see agencies like ours folding up because of reduced state and federal funding. It's unnecessary. I hope that what we're trying to do here can become a model for others—not necessarily our specific programs, but the fact that options for survival are plentiful. It's all a matter of attitude and determination."

chapter 3
ISSUES

T he growing involvement of nonprofit institutions in enterprise activities over the past decade raises many practical and profound issues. Legislators, tax and legal experts, community leaders, and the trustees, directors, and staff of nonprofits have all expressed their concern about the direction and implications of the well-established trend toward enterprise.

It seems clear to us from our survey of the sector that it is no longer (and never really has been) a question of *whether* enterprise has a place among nonprofits, but what kind of role it can and should play, what kinds of limits and constraints should be placed on it, what kinds of benefits and incentives can be applied to encourage its growth. Enterprise is already an important factor. It remains for those concerned in and outside the sector to determine how enterprise should continue to grow, in which direction, and to what degree.

This chapter outlines some of the issues raised by nonprofit enterprise as they are relevant to important constituencies: government policy makers; community leaders; funders; for-profit businesses; and nonprofit trustees, directors, staff, and clients. We have set out to define, as straightforwardly as possible, the present concerns of these constituencies and the issues that, we judge, will arise for them in the future. We touch upon issues pertaining strictly to the internal functioning of nonprofits and those that affect their place in the social and economic life of the community. We recognize that the relevance of any particular issue depends on such specific factors as the size of the community; the size, number, and types of nonprofits in the area and their existing enterprises; and the size and diversity of the local private sector.

As we see them, these issues can be divided roughly into attitudinal, philosophical, and practical considerations. Many of them, inevitably, overlap. Therefore, readers should refer to the sections that address their specific vantage point.

GOVERNMENT POLICYMAKERS

At federal, state, and local governmental policy-making levels, enterprise in the nonprofit sector is a complex issue, one that will not yield to simple answers or pat historical solutions.

Government must ask whether enterprise has any place at all in the nonprofit sector. If enterprise does have a role to play in funding nonprofits, government faces the even more complex and subtle task of defining in what manner and to what extent nonprofit enterprise should be encouraged.

Nonprofits have traditionally delivered goods and services deemed necessary (education, community development) or desirable (ballet, museums) for the public good. The government, in order to further the public good, has underwritten these efforts by providing direct and indirect subsidies through grants, tax exemptions, and incentives to private giving, some of which are extended to certain kinds of nonprofit enterprises. With the reduction of direct government subsidies, funding for these efforts in the nonprofit sector is potentially compromised. To continue to operate, nonprofits will either have to pursue other sources of donated funding or *create* revenue themselves, through enterprise, to replace lost subsidies.

The primary issue for government is the proper role of enterprise in the sector. As it stands today, laws and regulations both support and restrict nonprofit enterprise. They extend public support to these businesses, including the tax exemption for related business. They also stop far short of fully enabling the sector to generate wealth for its own support by taxing unrelated businesses. In some extreme cases, for instance, enterprise has jeopardized the parent nonprofit's tax-exempt status. As nonprofit enterprises grow in number and in size, the pressure grows for clear and consistent legislation and government regulations that will establish precisely the incentives and limits to enterprise in the nonprofit sector.

One can foresee great potential benefits for the sector from enterprise, especially if trends of less direct government funding and declining charitable contributions continue. A nonprofit sector dedicated to the public interest and capable of sustaining and supporting itself in some measure through enterprise would be an important step toward the democratization of philanthropy by shifting some control from a few wealthy donors. At the same time, the potential risks and problems cannot be overlooked. If a nonprofit generates significant income through enterprise, it in effect becomes more independent, not only of the policies and restrictions, but also of the donors, patrons, and clients of the organization itself and even of the community it was created to serve. It could become free to set its own policies, governed only by its board. Under these conditions, would continued governmental support (through tax exemptions) be justified?

Apocalyptic thinkers conjure up visions of a nonprofit behemoth, the size of IBM or Mobil Oil, for instance. Such an enterprise would enable its nonprofit parent to be "dangerously" independent, they argue, of the needs the nonprofit was established to serve, independent even of the tradition of service. They call on government to restrict enterprise.

In reality, the great majority of nonprofit enterprises are small businesses by nature and by their very natures are destined to remain so. First, the purpose of the nonprofit and the energies required to perform services will act as a brake, a self-limiting factor on the size of the enterprise. Second, without shareholders, with no ability to declare dividends or pay out profits, and with no way of using its equity, nonprofit enterprises have great difficulty attracting capital. Third, nonprofits are at a disadvantage in competing with for-profit firms for loans. Lending institutions want assets that can be attached, and they shy away from situations that might put them in the position of "closing down the orphanage." Fourth, nonprofit enterprises have a comparative disadvantage in attracting skilled management, being at present unable to offer talented managers a career path, compensation, or recognition comparable to that in the for-profit sector. The fifth limiting factor to nonprofit enterprise is the sector's inability to compete as single-mindedly or adaptively as for-profit firms. Finally, the very risk of enterprise is one less readily embraced by nonprofit enterprises, which are aware of the consequences of failure for the health and viability of their mission. Will they bet the museum on an enterprise? The charter and mission of nonprofits will restrain the board and the management. Risks will be minimized. Continuity is the treasured objective for nonprofits.

On the other end of the scale, some people see the sector in ruins, lured into the enterprise arena with the hope of easy money and destroyed by the odds against success that apply to all small businesses. There is a real paternal fear, expressed by many in and outside the sector, that without government protections, the nonprofit sector cannot survive as a business competitor. The paradox should be pointed out, however, that the same factors that limit the growth of nonprofit enterprises also protect them from extreme risk. Still, if the nonprofit sector is to continue to serve the public good, some thought must be given to protecting it from sudden bankruptcy.

At present, few nonprofits have exploited any significant share of their enterprise opportunities. In no small way, this reluctance to engage in enterprise can be laid at the door of confusing and often contradictory laws and regulations. (Part of the problem is attitudinal, to be sure. Few nonprofits understand statutes pertaining to tax liability, and many shy away from activities that might raise their visibility in IRS circles.) Inconsistent enforcement of tax codes, however, aggravates nonprofits' fears about entering the enterprise arena. When the IRS in one region rules that a certain kind of revenue-generating activity is related and therefore nontaxable, there is no guarantee that another regional IRS office, reviewing an almost identical case under the same guidelines, will hand down a similar ruling.

At the local level, the climate created by state and local governments has perhaps an even more dramatic day-to-day impact on nonprofit enterprise. It is beyond the scope of this report to detail the particular statutes in each state that have the most influence on the fortunes of nonprofit enterprises. But we would like to share some impressions and a rough assessment of some of the most prevalent problems.

To gather information on substance (alcohol and drug) abuse programs, letters were sent to the directors of each of the fifty relevant state agencies. The letter detailed the purposes of this survey and requested the agency's help in identifying organizations within the state that might be involved in some type of enterprise activity. We received responses from fewer than half the states. Of those, some states provided a substantial list of agencies that were operating revenue-generating enterprises. Others indicated that there did not seem to be anything pertinent to our inquiry in that state. Assuming that these agencies were established to deliver a similar range of services, we questioned why the climate for enterprise was so different from state to state.

One respondent, Charles M. Emmons, president of the Virginia Association of Drug Programs and assistant director of Project Jump Street in Richmond, pointed the finger at the state budgetary process. In some states, he explained, if a nonprofit generates unanticipated earned revenues, the state reduces by that amount the organization's allocation in the next year's budget. The effect of this procedure is to discourage enterprises and to encourage dependency on state funds. According to Emmons, this policy results in a kind of welfare-addicted organization: "Why go to work if all it will do is reduce your welfare payments and increase your costs?" Emmons continues: "With the knowledge that running an enterprise will be hard work, an additional strain on the staff, with a relatively small return particularly in the beginning, why would a nonprofit risk reducing a secure state allocation?" The budget policy of many states, he concludes, encourages a "tin cup mentality" and does not enable an organization to accumulate the needed capital to launch an enterprise.

States also affect nonprofit enterprises adversely by the sheer number of regulations to which they are subject. Most nonprofits are required to provide program delivery staff and client information. By adding enterprises, they substantially increase the record-keeping workload. Many agencies have had to hire full-time help just to comply with reporting regulatory requirements.

States place other obstacles in the path of nonprofits' self-sufficiency. For instance, several states make it difficult for nonprofits to own real estate, even their own offices or facilities. The laws may disallow nonprofits from using line items on their budgets for "facilities" to make mortgage payments. This rule has the effect of locking nonprofits into ever-increasing rental payments. In addition, it discourages nonprofits from improving facilities and makes it difficult for the organizations to move to better offices. These regulations, concludes Emmons, "convert *cash* to an *expense* versus an *asset.*"

Another problem at the state level can arise from state regulations of insurance companies. One source of income for social service agencies is reimbursements from third parties for services provided. However, counseling programs offered by these agencies are frequently ineligible for reimbursement from private insurers because insurers require the counseling to be provided by a Ph.D. or M.D.; but most counselors in social service agencies are M.S.W.'s. To help the agencies expand their earned income opportunities, states could require insurers to make reimbursements for services provided by qualified programs, regardless of the degree held by the individual counselor.

Many of these regulations, which discourage nonprofits from gaining some security through enterprise, owning appreciating assets, or broadening their potential market, encourage a dependency and a expense-oriented mentality. Such regulations were never designed to exert that kind of influence; they were designed to regulate other parts of the economy or to protect against a specific abuse and have ended up creating another in this new economic climate. The following questions and many others must be examined by government in order to define the proper role for nonprofit enterprise.

Enterprise and the nonprofit mission. Does enterprise belong in the nonprofit sector? To what extent should it be encouraged or constrained? Should government funds contribute either directly or indirectly to enterprise? If nonprofits become self-funding through enterprise, will they stop being responsive to the needs of the communities they were established to serve?

Regulatory role. What is the proper ongoing role for government to play in managing the development of nonprofit enterprise? Should it develop comprehensive policies or merely clean out the outdated legislative and executive "underbrush"? Should it extend the special protection enjoyed by nonprofits to include all of their enterprises? What additional provisions need to be made for periodic review and monitoring of the sector? Should the IRS continue to fulfill this function?

Abuse of enterprise. Should the nonprofit sector be given a clear "license" to engage in enterprise? What possible misuses or abuses are likely to occur from such licensing? Will tax-exempt status be used to shelter for-profit income? How can abuses be prevented?

Protection for nonprofit businesses. If nonprofit enterprises operate in a completely free-market environment, are they assuming risks that might put their parent nonprofits in jeopardy? Is it necessary or fair to shelter nonprofit businesses from the open market? To what extent? Is the pursuit of enterprise realistic only if it can survive in the same environment as for-profits?

Failure of nonprofit enterprises. Does governmental support for enterprise imply a parallel responsibility to provide financial relief or to ease the collapse of the inevitable business failures (as in the for-profit sector)? What value would a Small Business Administration for nonprofits provide?

Use of profits. Should the use of profits generated by these enterprises (other than the already-in-force constraint of distributing profits) be limited by legislation?

Unrelated business income. Should a review be conducted of the regulations regarding "unrelated business income"? Can (or should) consistent national standards be established to clear up current inconsistencies?

Enterprise tax. If nonprofits are "licensed" to conduct enterprise, should they be taxed on non-program-related income? At the same rate as for-profit enterprises?

Incentives/disincentives. In addition to tax laws, what other incentives or disincentives can state and federal governments offer to nonprofit enterprises?

Climate for enterprise. What specific state and local regulations influence the ability of nonprofits to undertake enterprise activities? What, if any, regulations should be changed?

On a national or state level, nonprofit enterprise is an issue of policy, but on a city or community level, the issues are more practical and immediate. Nonprofits are an important part of a community's self-image, its history, and its tradition of philanthropy. The community thus has clear-cut (if unspoken) expectations of how its nonprofits should behave, whom they should serve, and how and by whom they should be supported and controlled.

COMMUNITY LEADERSHIP

Specific legal and regulatory considerations, limits, incentives, and disincentives are complex issues, but it is our impression, on the basis of interviews and surveys, that the complexities of attitude and relationships among nonprofits and between them and the communities they serve are the more important and difficult issues.

If a community's nonprofits deliver valuable services, and if they, in common with most of their peers, are experiencing a funding crisis, community leaders must ask themselves whether it is in the best interests of the town and of the nonprofits themselves to create a climate of law and opinion within which nonprofit enterprise can flourish. Are enterprise-generated revenues necessary or desirable sources of funding for nonprofits? Can the town afford nontaxable businesses, and if so, how many? If nonprofits are restricted from generating revenue through enterprise, where will program funds be raised? If enterprise is encouraged, what will happen to those nonprofits who cannot or will not engage in enterprise? As cutbacks in federal funding occur, not only for many nonprofits but also for cities themselves, these questions have become more pressing for local leadership. Assuming local government funds cannot make up for the federal shortfall, the pressure on local contributors—foundations, corporations, and individuals—will inevitably increase. As some funders have already experienced in the wake of federal cuts, solicitations from nonprofits can multiply many times over. Especially in communities with strong traditions of philanthropy, having to say no to these funding requests is never easy.

Many of the attitudinal constraints represent fears that various members of the community have about what a movement toward enterprise will mean. Will enterprises run out of the control of the community? Will local donors lose their importance to the organization? Will nonprofits focus on their businesses to the exclusion of service? Will they lose touch with the needs of the community? Will they enter into competition with local businesses? Will they compete fairly or will they use their tax advantages to the detriment of the business community? From our survey we would argue that these fears do not reflect the reality of the vast majority of nonprofit enterprises. Even those nonprofits we interviewed that were most involved in enterprise activities were as fully aware of their obligations to serve as any of their colleagues.

On the more practical side, local leaders must consider in dollars and cents what nonprofit enterprise will mean for competing for-profits and for the city or town coffers, too. The sad reality is that many towns, especially in the older eastern section of the nation, cannot afford to overlook potential tax dollars. One city in the Northeast has even tried to levy a "service fee" on tax-exempt nonprofits. The nonprofits have refused and the city has responded by going to the public with its plight, making nonprofits appear greedy and uncaring.

Enterprise raises the visibility of nonprofits, for good or ill. Enterprises that generate the revenue to increase services perceptibly (e.g., to expand the number of low-income clients served in a mental health program) can increase community pride in the whole nonprofit sector. But if, for instance, a residential rehabilitation center starts a bakery using in-house labor and drives a for-profit baker in the area out of business, the negative repercussions would be felt in both sectors. Even if the nonprofit sets up the bakery as an unrelated business and therefore pays taxes on income, the competitor might charge "unfair" competition based on the fact that the tax-exempt center has lower costs and pays no real estate or other local taxes. In a particularly acrimonious case, the charge of unfair competition might stick to all local nonprofits as opposed to only enterprises.

How the role of nonprofit enterprise is defined and managed within the community will depend on these and other factors:

- [ ] **Community pride:** What effect will nonprofit enterprise have on the tradition of community service? How will attitudes or enterprises change?
- [ ] **Control:** What local limits, if any, should the community exercise or institute over the size and kinds of nonprofit enterprises?
- [ ] **Attitude of city fathers:** Will the attitude of this group (which tends to include not only the leaders in government, but also the board members and main supporters of local nonprofits) lead to a climate hostile or favorable to enterprise? How do the city fathers see their roles changing with respect to the community and to the relevant nonprofit with the advent of enterprise?
- [ ] **Funding sources:** If enterprise generates significant income for nonprofits, what role will local donors (corporate and individual) have to play?
- [ ] **Visibility:** If one nonprofit launches a highly visible enterprise, how will it affect other nonprofits (even those without any enterprise activities) in the community? How can nonprofits with enterprise activities both capitalize and preserve the good name of the whole sector?
- [ ] **Responsiveness:** If nonprofits succeed in funding themselves through enterprise, and consequently depend less directly on the community, what guarantees are necessary to ensure that nonprofits remain responsive to changing community needs?
- [ ] **Private sector relations:** Will local business leaders be concerned about the implications of enterprise ventures as a source of funding? What factors will influence them either to support or to resist enterprise?
- [ ] **Competition:** Will nonprofit enterprises enter into competition with local for-profit businesses? How will these competitors react, and which will the community support? How will a competitive struggle affect the local climate of opinion and the image of nonprofits in the community?

BUSINESS COMMUNITY

If nonprofits become more aggressively entrepreneurial, they will inevitably step on some toes in the business community; it is conceivable that they might even do more serious harm.

The growth of nonprofit enterprise can create opportunities for small business as well as intensify competition. In fact, much of nonprofit enterprise—such as the manufacture of tote bags and T-shirts with the nonprofit name or logo, licensing of reproductions—is already very profitable for the business community. Joint ventures with nonprofit partners as a trend is growing and encompassing more ambitious and far-reaching projects, such as the development of office parks and shopping centers and long-term licensing and marketing arrangements.

Despite the evidence of opportunity for for-profit business in nonprofit enterprise, it is the issue of competition and risk that is most discussed and debated.

Basically, nonprofit enterprise can put the business community at risk in three ways: as market competitors, as donors, and as competitors for personnel.

First, and by far the most volatile, is the issue of competition for markets. To quote from a speech given to the National Council on Philanthropy by John G. Simon, director of the Program on Non-Profit Organizations at Yale University:

> . . . most of these nonprofit vs. for-profit competitive situations are far from truly amicable. The landscape is dotted with commercial firms—research firms, travel agencies, professional service firms, etc.—that are suing or lobbying or just plain screaming about the nonprofit firms that are said to be "unfairly" competing with them with the help of the law—tax exemptions, favorable postal rates, favorable pension laws, and the preferences for nonprofits that are built into all kinds of government grant and contract programs.

There is an undoubted tension between the tax and legal preferences and incentives applied by the government to the nonprofit sector and the rules of fair competition in the marketplace. Until these issues are clarified at the government level, the question of fairness in competition will have to be argued case by case. It should be noted that competition puts both parties at risk: Not only do for-profit businesses risk markets, but so do nonprofits. Nonprofits additionally put their good name and possibly tax status at risk in an all-out competitive battle. Fortunately, there are alternatives to head-on competition under less than equal circumstances. Many nonprofits sensibly choose enterprises that will not put them in direct competition with a local business, or else they enlist business partners in joint ventures. But it should be noted that successful enterprise breeds its own competitors, and not even the most careful strategic planning on the part of a nonprofit can shield enterprises from the conflicts of the marketplace. However, the more cooperation that takes place between for-profit and nonprofit enterprises, the fewer incidents of unfair competition should occur.

Second, businesses contribute substantially to the support of nonprofits. In addition to straight cash and in-kind contributions, many businesses have proud traditions of service, including employee volunteer programs, executive loan programs, trusteeships, and so on.

Some believe that these programs are threatened by enterprise: The satisfaction of giving either money or time to a worthy cause will be replaced by impersonal businesslike transactions, buying the products or services of a nonprofit at fair market value.

The third question is the competition for personnel. Any business the nonprofit enters requires skills that have probably been gained in the private sector. Therefore, it is inevitable, in a world of scarce, skilled human resources, that the two sectors will be competing for these resources. The weapon in the battle will undoubtedly be compensation. It remains to be seen whether the nonprofit parent will be able to keep up or whether some new forms of noncash compensation, such as policy-making authority or work environment factors, can be effective counterbalances.

Other concerns include the following.

☐ **Relations with the nonprofit sector:** Are relations between local businesses and nonprofits generally strong or weak? Does the business community support nonprofits primarily with cash contributions? In-kind contributions? Employee volunteer or lend-lease programs? Technical expertise? Positions on the board? Purchasing or using nonprofit services? How might enterprise alter this relationship?

☐ **Contributions:** Is the primary link between the business and nonprofit sectors cash contributions? How will these contributions be affected by nonprofit enterprises? Will the business community be willing and able to give to enterprise as well as to programs? What new kinds of contribution opportunities are created by enterprise? In-kind contributions of planning, marketing, or distribution skills, for instance, or executives on loan?

☐ **Competition:** What kinds of enterprises will local nonprofits undertake? Will they directly compete with existing businesses?

☐ **Joint ventures:** Could some nonprofit enterprises be more profitable (to both sectors) if managed as joint ventures? Would joint ventures be undertaken as a profit opportunity for the corporation or as an indirect contribution? Is it important which partner proposes the marriage?

☐ **Taxes:** Will these enterprises pay taxes on unrelated income, or will they be ruled related to the nonprofit's mission? How will the tax issue affect competition and corporate contributions?

FUNDERS

Increased enterprise activity will alter in some measure the relationship between nonprofits and funders—the foundations, corporations, and individuals who support them. With enterprise providing revenues for some nonprofits, new options and choices will arise for funders.

Exactly how enterprise will influence granting policies and procedures is not yet known. Funders are such a diverse group, each with specific charter restrictions, available levels of funding, and traditions of support and outlook, that generalizations are difficult.

As funders, what is the appropriate response to enterprise? Some of course have and will continue to ignore enterprise simply because, for many funders, it lies outside the charter of the organization. For the rest, enterprise presents an addition to an already full roster of programs and organizations worthy of support, complicating grant review procedures and relationships with grantees.

If a funding organization decides to support nonprofit enterprise, the questions then arise concerning in what manner and to what extent it should do so. Corporate, foundation, and individual funders are already painfully aware of their inabilities to support valuable yet hard-pressed nonprofits. Enterprise, while it does add to the lengthy list of grant applications, does provide a new way in which funders can *leverage* their contributions to the sector. It is quite possible that a one-time investment of seed capital in a nonprofit enterprise will yield returns that support program services for years to come. Considered in this light, funders might see enterprise as a mechanism through which they could in the long term provide incentives for self-sufficiency in the sector. Yet even this exciting possibility raises problems for funders. What kind of funding should be allocated to enterprise? Straight grants? Interest-free loans? "Model enterprise" grants? Program-related investment? What kind of limits and restrictions to funding should be applied? Should funders, for instance, give grants of seed capital for "unrelated" and therefore taxable businesses? Should only related enterprises be considered? Should enterprise grants carry limitations on the use of profits (for maintenance support, a specific program, or for funds to further self-sufficiency)?

Enterprise will create new nonprofit haves and have-nots. There will be organizations that will grow and prosper by wisely exploiting their enterprise opportunities, and there will be others that for a variety of reasons cannot and should not engage in enterprise. Funders who choose to support enterprise will have to decide to what extent they will support each of these two groups. What share of funding will be set aside for programs, maintenance, and support and what share for enterprise? Will separate standards for review have to be established for the two groups?

Perhaps the most delicate problem raised by enterprise is how the nonprofit community will perceive a funder's support for enterprise. Will the funder be criticized for abandoning programs? How will the relationship between funders and the communities they serve (including both the grantee nonprofits and their clients) change? Will enterprise grants enable funders to help nonprofits meet the current crisis in funding or create bad feelings?

As a final note, currently many nonprofits drag their feet on enterprise, believing that if they are able to generate income themselves, they might alienate funders. It is our impression from the interviews we conducted with nonprofit directors that many are waiting for funders to give the green light to enterprise. (This answers in part the objection raised by some funders that enterprise will reduce their policy role.)

The following list details funders' more practical concerns with enterprise.

☐ *Funding enterprise:* Should funders support enterprise or restrict gifts to programs only?

☐ *Supporting "haves" and "have-nots":* On what basis, if any, should funders distinguish between nonprofits that can and do contribute to their own support through enterprise and those that are not able to do so? What about nonprofits that either cannot or choose not to engage in enterprise or those that fail at enterprise activities?

☐ *Giving versus investment:* Should some funding be set aside as seed capital for building self-sufficient organizations rather than contributions to operating funds? Will "return on investment" become a term relevant to funders? What will this mean to the philosophy of giving and to the sector?

☐ *Funders' policy role:* If contributions form a less significant part of the nonprofit sector's income, will funders have less "say" in policy, in the direction of the sector and the services it provides?

TRUSTEES

For board members with responsibilities in the community and also fiduciary responsibility for the nonprofit, enterprise is a double-edged sword. While it may take up slack in funding, enterprise also puts the organization at risk and affects the nonprofit's position in the community with respect to its funders and patrons, clients, and fellow nonprofit and for-profit entities.

The day-to-day operational problems raised by enterprise are the province of nonprofit management, but it falls to trustees to determine and ratify the direction of change. As members in good standing of the community and in many cases as "city fathers," they must not only weigh the options with the interests of the organization in mind but also consider the external environment. As such, the first question to be addressed by trustees is whether enterprise is a necessary or desirable option for the nonprofit, and to what extent the option can be exercised without violating the terms of the unwritten contract between the community and the nonprofit. Enterprise will inevitably raise the nonprofit's visibility in the community. In some communities, for instance, a strong civic tradition of charity might perceive enterprise as "creeping commercialism." In other cases, it is the nature of the nonprofit itself that will determine how readily its enterprises are accepted. For instance, a younger, more aggressive social service agency might have a wider franchise for enterprise than one of the community's oldest cultural institutions, which the leading citizens have always taken pride in supporting through individual corporate contributions. Also, the kind of enterprise chosen will affect community reaction. A museum bookstore, even when professionally run and highly profitable, may be more acceptable to the community than a dry-cleaning plant, for instance. Another important part of the contract between the nonprofit and the community is the business sector. Cries of "unfair competition" from for-profit firms can adversely affect enterprise if the parent nonprofit does not adequately consider its responsbility to its neighbors in the business community.

The move into enterprise not only raises organizational visibility, it also increases risk for the nonprofit. Small businesses are risky ventures, and trustees, as those responsible for the fiduciary interests of the nonprofit, must carefully balance these risks against the need for prudence, to conserve the organization's resources. Trustees must evaluate not only the business venture and its chances for survival or possible success, but also the enterprise's impact on programs and mission, on contributions, and on the perception of the nonprofit in the community.

First, of course, the trustees must evaluate the business venture's chances for success. Not only is this the proper role of trustees, but in most nonprofits it is at the trustee level where the necessary business talent and expertise exist. Is the nonprofit staff competent to design and run a business venture? Will entrepreneurs/managers have to be recruited from outside? How will the entrepreneurs be integrated into (and accepted by) the rest of the organization? Beyond examining the business plan and management concerns, trustees must be concerned with what kind of drain on the organization the enterprise will represent. Can the enterprise be managed without draining funds or human resources from programs or services?

The kind of enterprise planned raises trustee-level questions of tax and legal considerations. Will the enterprise generate "unrelated" business income? What will this mean to the tax status of the nonprofit? Not only will tax issues become more complicated, but also as boundaries between sectors are approached, waters become more troubled.

One kind of risk that disturbs the trustees of many nonprofits is what enterprise will mean to contributions. The pervasive fear that enterprise and contributions are alternatives in a zero-sum game is not borne out by our study. Although the concern that enterprise might discourage contributors was raised again and again, it was raised by those who had *no* experience with enterprise beyond the level of the volunteer-run bookstore or gift shop. The experience of nonprofits that do engage in enterprise and that manage their enterprises as businesses, not services, is that contributions do not drop off in significant measure.

For instance, Stanford University and Princeton University, both of which have been involved in multimillion-dollar land development ventures, have reported an increase in contributions since initiating their enterprise activities. Sports are an important revenue-generating enterprise for many colleges, but a winning team does not cost the school contributions. It would be difficult to prove that contributions to New York's Metropolitan Museum of Art suffer because it is a large, wealthy, and powerful institution. On a smaller scale, the Denver Children's Museum (see the case study in chapter 2), which generates 95 percent of its income, continues to attract contributions. As a general rule, success does not cost a nonprofit support any more than failure attracts it. Instead, the adage "success follows success" applies.

Saying no to enterprise may be more difficult if the trend toward enterprise continues. The pressure to jump on the bandwagon will be felt particularly in the boardroom. What will it mean to the organization if there are no opportunities for enterprise? Or if it is unable or unwilling to take advantage of the opportunities that do exist?

Finally, it should be noted that levels of nonprofit board involvement range widely from day-to-day attention to operations to more distant planning. The questions that follow highlight the considerations that most trustees will address in assessing enterprise.

- [ ] *"Role" of the nonprofit:* Will enterprise change the community's attitude—and possibly its support—of nonprofits? Is enterprise inimical to service?
- [ ] *Tradition:* Will enterprise be seen as a violation of the traditional role of the nonprofit? How can the way be prepared to make enterprise an acceptable option for the community?
- [ ] *Management of the organization:* Is the nonprofit equipped internally to manage an enterprise, to develop a business plan, and to run a new small business that has a chance to succeed? If entrepreneurial skills are not available in house, where can the nonprofit acquire these skills? Are these skills available from board members? Are they willing and able to contribute them? If entrepreneurs are hired, how will they be integrated into the organization? How will they be compensated? What effect will an in-house entrepreneur have on the morale and compensation of other members of the staff?
- [ ] *Risk of enterprise:* Does enterprise put undue stress on the fiscal condition of the nonprofit? How can the inevitable risks of a new business be kept at a manageable level? What would happen to the nonprofit if the business failed?

□ **Seed capital:** How will the money to fund an enterprise be raised? Will it compromise program funding efforts for program delivery?

□ **Enterprise versus program:** Will engaging in enterprise draw needed resources (human and financial) away from programs?

□ **Relationship with funders:** What effect will launching an enterprise have on the nonprofit's funders?

□ **Relationship with local businesses:** How will the community's for-profit concerns react to enterprise?

□ **Tax issues:** Will the enterprise generate "unrelated" or related income? How will this affect the organization? Do trustees have sufficient understanding of tax implications?

EXECUTIVE DIRECTORS

The immediate responsibility for launching a nonprofit enterprise in most cases falls to the organization's directors. It is their task not only to evaluate the potential gain and risk involved in enterprise, but also to manage the complex and subtle changes that inevitably will affect the organizational structure in its wake.

As the stewards of the organizations they head, executive directors must first consider the implications of enterprise for the nonprofit's mission and, equally important, of the community's perception of its mission. As discussed in other parts of this chapter, in some cases the community at large, as well as trustees, funders, staff, and even clients of the nonprofits, may consider enterprise as inappropriate at best. These perceptions and the attitudes that lie behind them are crucial to the position of the nonprofit in the community, its ability to raise funds, and the eventual success or failure of enterprises.

It is the executive director who (with the board) must decide whether enterprise is an option for the organization, and, if so, how the option can be realized. For example, should the enterprise function only as a generator of revenue (and if so, how much), or must it also meet a further agenda of employing or serving clients?

In any case, enterprise presents a stiff challenge to executive directors. Most are already stretched to the limit with demands on their time and talent. Organizing and preparing the way for enterprise and managing the changes that follow in its wake, in addition to managerial, administrative, and program duties, may be more than an executive director can handle.

The choices fall to the director: Is enterprise a viable option for the organization? As part of its mission or part of a movement toward self-sufficiency? If enterprise is not an option now, does it have a place in the organization's future? How can enterprise be presented to the community in order to attract its support? Who will run the enterprise?

Many of the outstanding examples of enterprise identified in this study are run by directors/entrepreneurs. Yet, they are the exceptions to the rule. For a gifted nonprofit director to try to take on entrepreneurial responsibilities for which he or she has no training or background is as unrealistic as to suppose the president of Mobil Oil could be a successful wildcatter. They are separate skills, rarely coexisting in the same person. As enterprise becomes a more normative experience in the nonprofit sector, hiring entrepreneurial talent will become more common as well.

It will fall to directors to manage the organizational changes that follow from enterprise. The daily life and outlook of the organization will be altered, however subtly. How can an entrepreneur be integrated into the nonprofit structure? Will enterprise and program staff cooperate or conflict? Should they be compensated on the same scale? How close a control over the operations of the enterprise should director and board exert? What will enterprise mean to the tax and legal status of the nonprofit?

Particularly in the boardroom, the tax ramifications seem to raise barriers to new enterprise ventures. The barriers are in no small measure attitudinal, but these attitudes are based on a thirty-year history of complex modifications, court tests, and reversals in tax legislation and in wide variations in local rulings that have made many wary of activities that might bring them under the close scrutiny of the IRS. But our survey of enterprising nonprofits indicates that successful entrepreneurs make a practice of consulting the local IRS office about enterprise plans, using IRS expertise to help design the right entity.

The questions that enterprise raises for the executive director are myriad, ranging from philosophical concerns of mission to practical details of accounting:

☐ *Community attitudes:* How will the community react to enterprise? How will the climate of opinion affect the enterprise's chances of success?

☐ *Trustee attitudes:* Will the board support the enterprise option? How will enterprise affect board members' position vis-a-vis the community and its leaders, funding sources, and so on?

☐ *Staff and volunteer attitudes:* How will the staff react to enterprise? How will volunteers be affected? Will a more businesslike orientation change existing volunteer-run enterprises?

☐ *Selection of enterprise:* If enterprise is an option, what kind of enterprise should be undertaken? Who should be assigned to evaluate possible enterprises and develop business plans?

☐ *Management:* Who will manage the enterprise? Are the needed skills available on the staff or among the board members? If not, where will they be found? If an entrepreneur is hired, how will he or she fit in with the staff? How will he or she be received by the board? How will the entrepreneur be compensated? How will this addition affect compensation rates for (and consequently attitudes of) other staff members?

☐ **Financial and accounting:** What changes in accounting procedures will be required to manage an enterprise properly? Where will the seed capital to launch the enterprise be raised? Will this compromise sources for program funding? Are the organization's present cash management practices sufficient to take on the additional requirements of enterprise? Will the enterprise require instituting practices that influence the efficiency of the rest of the organization?

☐ **Setting of goals:** What size of enterprise is appropriate for the organization? What levels of income are necessary or desirable? To what extent is the enterprise purely a generator of revenue and to what extent is it designed to fulfill other purposes, such as employing or serving clients and offering services to patrons, donors, or members?

☐ **Mission:** Will the running of an enterprise detract from the image or compromise the mission of the organization?

☐ **Taxes:** How will the organization be affected if the enterprise generates "unrelated" (taxable) business income? Is this enterprise in a gray area, not clearly related or unrelated until determined by an IRS ruling? What is the organization's relationship with the local IRS office? How will this affect the enterprise?

☐ **Competition:** Will the enterprise compete with already established local businesses? How would this competition affect the nonprofit's relationship with the community, local businesses, or the IRS? Is a joint venture with a for-profit partner a viable alternative to an independent enterprise?

☐ **Clients:** How will clients perceive and be affected by an enterprise?

PERSONNEL

Enterprise will mean changes for the staffs of nonprofits. The staff members of enterprises tend to make their career choices for different motivations than do employees in nonprofit organizations. In enterprising nonprofits where these groups of people mingle, certain tensions are bound to surface. In many ways, these tensions are similar to those between line and staff in a corporation. (In this case, the program staff members see themselves as line and the enterprise group as staff.)

When a nonprofit initiates enterprise, it may violate an unspoken agreement with employees by "tainting" its mission with the practices and values of business. If the nonprofit does not clearly position enterprise as a mechanism to generate revenue for services, enterprise may be perceived as a threat to the values of the institution and sector.

Employees will ask themselves if they want to work for an organization involved in enterprise or if they would rather work for one that directs all its energies to programs? They may legitimately prefer to work for an organization that *asks* for money rather than one that *earns* it. The change in attitude necessary to accept enterprise is not an easy one for staff to make, particularly if they have not been included in planning the enterprise.

Beyond questions of attitude, enterprise raises practical questions of compensation. How will the enterprise staff be compensated? If non-profit enterprises are managed as businesses, then it is to be expected that their staffs will be compensated like counterparts in the for-profit sector. Otherwise, it will be impossible to recruit and retain the best personnel. (One energy-related nonprofit in the Northwest, for instance, has had to employ incentive compensation for its energy auditors because of intense competition for people with these skills from for-profit firms in their market.) But with separate and unequal pay scales for program and enterprise staff, the program staff will be perceived as less "valuable," at least in monetary terms. Our survey shows this tension to be inevitable at this time. The solutions, if any, to this problem will have to be found within each organization.

In any discussion of the impact of enterprise on nonprofits, volunteers must hold a special place. In our survey we found many (in number if not in income) nonprofit enterprises staffed and managed by volunteers. More frequently than we had expected, enterprises were the brain-children of a particularly committed volunteer or group of volunteers. Often, in the transition to a more professional management, nonprofits have shifted these enterprises (gift shops, bookstores, walking tours, publications, etc.) from volunteer to staff control while continuing to use volunteer workers to keep overhead low. Thus many of these dedicated volunteers perceive themselves as having much to lose from enterprise. Staff who are dependent on volunteer support to deliver client services are also concerned about the possible loss of this valuable (if unpaid) resource. It would indeed be ironic if nonprofit businesses were managed in such a way as to disenfranchise this group, which perhaps more than any other has pioneered the cause of enterprise in the nonprofit sector, without identifying a suitable alternative channel for its talents. The following questions should be asked in this regard:

☐ *Professional identification:* How will program workers, who identify themselves professionally with the nonprofit sector and their particular discipline (such as curator or social worker) react when the organization becomes a "business"? Will the enterprise staff identify itself equally with the nonprofit mission?

☐ *Volunteers and enterprise:* If the enterprise is an existing volunteer-run activity (such as a bookstore or gift shop), will volunteers be displaced by professional staff? How will this change affect the morale? How will it affect the ability of the program staff to attract volunteers to the organization?

☐ *Enterprise staff:* How will the enterprise staff accept or gain the acceptance of the program staff?

☐ *Compensation:* Should the enterprise staff be compensated on the same basis as its colleagues in the profit sector or its fellow nonprofit staff members? How will the enterprise attract talented staff if it cannot compensate them as for-profit firms would? What will be the effect of having program and enterprise staff compensated on two different scales?

chapter 4

ORGANIZATIONAL
SELF-EVALUATION

T|||||||| his chapter is written for the trustees, directors, and staff members of nonprofits that are standing on the threshold of enterprise, considering a first venture or adding to a roster of existing business activities, managing the expansion of a particularly successful enterprise, or looking for inventive ways to reduce costs. Even those who are not considering the enterprise option may find the chapter useful in planning.

What follows is neither a business plan nor a prescription. Enterprise is not a patent cure. It is, however, an exercise in thinking constructively about enterprise opportunities. This chapter follows the process of planning through the initial stages, from raising the question of enterprise to pinpointing one or two actual businesses most appropriate for a particular nonprofit. Readers must bring to this chapter a level of self-knowledge as well as a willingness to test their assumptions, to think hard, and to work in painstaking detail. In return, the questions will lead readers through the process of examining the opportunities for and limits to enterprise and its management and financial issues to the point of choosing the right enterprise(s) for their particular organization and whether to proceed or not. Often, deciding to refrain from exercising the enterprise option is the most profitable choice.

This chapter is organized in sections, each asking a series of questions. The questions are based on the experience of hundreds of nonprofit enterprises, comprising a range of 501(c)(3) organizations. Not surprisingly, then, not all questions apply to all organizations; readers will want to adapt them to their own needs.

1. *Should your organization be involved in enterprise?*

Small businesses have a way of being romanticized as part of the American dream or the foundation of a legendary fortune. The reality is that small businesses demand constant care and close attention, and in the end, 90 percent of them fail within the first 10 years.

Before you even consider enterprise seriously, this fact should be firmly in mind: Some nonprofits *should not* venture into enterprise; others *cannot*. A nonprofit nursing home, for instance, might not have the kind of markets, labor, or resources that can be turned to business. In addition, its main program, the care of the ailing and elderly, is a demanding task and one from which capital and human resources cannot comfortably be diverted.

Whether your organization should undertake enterprise at all is the first and most important question. It should be asked and answered not just initially, but time and again during the course of assessing your resources and planning possible business activities.

2. *Assets: What do you have to work with?*

Make a complete list of your organization's assets, both tangible and intangible.

This exercise is easy to state, but difficult and time-consuming to accomplish. Take your time. Do some research. When you have exhausted the obvious, be imaginative. Above all, don't overlook anything by relying simply on the balance sheet.

A. *Tangible assets:*
What do you own or have the right to use? The following list of tangible assets will help you get started:
- [ ] Real estate (land, buildings), property rights and natural resources (mineral, water, timber, and even air rights)
- [ ] Equipment (office, maintenance, special program-related equipment)

  library
  printshop
  laboratory

  (It may help to make a list of the organization's activities first, then backtrack through a list of equipment necessary to carry out the activities.)
- [ ] Valuable items (museum collection, musical instruments, etc.; cash, cash equivalents, unrestricted endowment)

B. *People—talent and expertise:*
Who works for your organization? Are you aware of all their skills and talents? How much skilled and unskilled labor is available on staff and in the community? Do you have a large

pool of willing volunteers? A staff with highly developed and specialized technical or managerial skills? What about board skills? What expertise is available in the community? Don't stop with a list of skills your organization recognizes and uses. Disc Village found a licensed optician on staff who provided an excellent entree into the optical business. Pull out resumes and read them carefully. Interview staffers, volunteers, and board members. What business skills and experience do they have and at what level? Are there talented volunteers who might be interested in full-time paid employment?

Analyzing your organization's human resources and those readily accessible outside the organization is one of the most critical exercises in this chapter. By examining in detail how much labor is available to your organization and at what skill levels, you may identify some logical enterprise opportunities. Consider these examples: Perhaps the professional staff of your organization has developed an innovative and very successful counseling program. These are unique skills, and they represent an opportunity for the organization to develop, publish, and sell a handbook or become consultants on how to run such a program. Or perhaps your organization has a large pool of volunteers who conduct tours of your facility. These same volunteers may be excellent cooks, capable of supplying the skilled labor for an on-site restaurant or of contributing their expertise to the publication of a cookbook.

C. *Traffic:*

Who comes to you? Who comes by you? Traffic is an often overlooked asset. Once you understand the stream of traffic through your organization, how many come to you and how long they spend at your location, enterprise opportunities will occur to you. Can you attach conclusions to the stream a la Disneyland—food tours, shops, souvenirs? What other kinds of activities would your visitors be interested in? Perhaps you are visited by a steady stream of scholars and researchers who would be interested in a computer bibliographic service. Or, perhaps they would be willing to give guest lectures to visitors or as a part of a course. You must first know exactly who uses your organization—visitors, members, scholars and researchers, the ill, handicapped, or elderly? Do you attract large numbers of people? You will need numbers, a demographic breakdown, and an idea of when they come. Are your clients/ patrons/visitors young or old, rich or poor, male or female, professional or blue-collar, employed or unemployed? Zoos, for instance, have a steady stream of youngsters and families; art museums have a different clientele, including adult visitors and scholars. If your organization does not have the information, suggest a survey of traffic be taken. You should also find out, if possible, what kind of traffic moves *around* your facility, that is, who comes *by* but not *in*.

D. *Facilities:*

What facilities does your organization own or lease? This is more than a simple listing of properties. Does it have access to office space, gallery, dormitory, inn rooms, kitchen, auditorium, gardens, conference hall, parking lot, warehouse, laboratories? Include all facilities, whether or not the organization fully utilizes them at present. Also, take a survey of your neighborhood to see if you might be able to use neighborhood facilities. One drug treatment program in Seattle bought a nearby vacant lot to house its recycling plant.

E. *Patents and licenses:*

If your organization has patents or patentable research, you most likely know about it. The unexploited patent, like the family heirloom that turns out to be a valuable antique, is more legend than fact. However, more and more nonprofits find that they possess designs (everything from china to textiles to a design for a drug rehabilitation program) that can be licensed, patented, or published profitably for reproduction and sale.

F. *Time:*

Referring to your inventory of equipment, facilities, and talent, *when* specifically does your organization use these assets? When *aren't* you using them? Nights and weekends? Are there slack months or seasons? *Downtime*—people, facilities, or equipment—can be a valuable enterprise asset. You may find on staff a pool of talent used fully only at certain times during the year—during a fund drive, for instance. This pool may be the human capital that's needed to form a new business. There may be rooms, buildings, land, or equipment that could be rented out to others. In addition to targeting potential enterprise opportunities, the analysis can also help you look at asset utilization and possible cost cuts. For instance, as a cost-reduction measure, you might consider replacing underutilized staff with freelance talent on an as-needed basis.

G. *Allies:*

Who are your friends outside the organization? Most nonprofits have influential allies—trustees and funders, for instance—who are leaders in the community. At the grassroots level, members are also allies, as are the families of clients.

In this exercise of who-do-you-know, it would be useful to prepare a membership breakdown for your organization. Include numbers and demographics. Who are your members? Where do they live? How do they earn their living? What other activities do they enjoy (besides supporting your organization)?

Also, list your trustees and, most important, individual and corporate contributors and the families of those you serve. Again, look at the demographics and do some research. Who are they? What other community services do they support? Who are their contacts?

H. *Reputation:*

Your good name is also an asset. It means something in the community, but *what* does it mean and to whom? Are you an accepted source of knowledge on art, natural history, music, dance, children? What kind of products or services does this expertise suggest? A dance company, in addition to being accepted experts on performance, also has expertise in dance wear, shoes, staging, lighting, etc. A symphony's expertise in music is often used in recording. A children's museum, a zoo, or museum of natural history are experts on their young audiences. This expertise could be turned to publishing children's books or magazines, for instance, where its name would make a difference.

Your reputation is both an asset and a liability. The good name of the local Public Broadcasting Service (PBS) station, for instance, silkscreened on a tote bag makes the bag worth something to public television supporters. On the other hand, your good name limits the kind of business your constituents would support. For instance, the good name of the local art museum would be of no value in the manufacture of lead pipe. In fact, it might even be a liability.

Try to determine exactly what your organization's good name means. Is yours an image of quiet quality, relentless pursuit of justice, etc.? For whom is this image important? Members and clients only? The community at large? As a note of caution, test your assumptions about your organizational image with an objective outsider. Often the image of an organization is something quite different inside the organization than it is to the community at large. And often enterprise can make a positive contribution to image. One drug rehabilitation program made and sold cheesecakes for a while in its community. Residential clients baked them in the house kitchen. When the group stopped this activity, it found that the community at large had developed a positive image of the organization because of the cheesecake business.

You now have several lists that represent your organizational assets in the widest possible sense. Now review these lists, looking for your comparative advantage: That is, what assets does your organization have (or have access to) that no other nonprofit or business in your community has? If others have the same assets, are there unique "extras" that give your organization the advantage? What sorts of enterprises could be built using these resources?

3. Market opportunities

An American living in London stopped in a stationery store and asked for a particular item. The shopkeeper said they didn't carry it, but added, "You know, we get a dozen requests a week for that item." The American asked if it ever occurred to him to stock the item. "No," he replied, "that's not on our lists."

That is a parable of a missed market opportunity. If your organization is asked week after week about some item, that may tell you something important about market needs and opportunities. It might be useful, therefore, for someone in the organization to undertake to document what kinds of requests are made every week by staff members, bookstore or gift shop clerks, guides, and people who staff information booths. What is your market asking for that you don't provide, but might be able to? In short, do some market research.

American business men and women have the reputation of actively looking for opportunities and following them up when things look promising. The same curiosity and initiative can be beneficial in targeting market opportunities for nonprofits.

Nonprofits serve several markets: clients, members, patrons, the community at large. A nonprofit enterprise has a comparative advantage in these markets because the good name and reputation of the parent nonprofit means most to these people.

Learn as much as you can about these people: They are your most logical target market, although they may not be the only market you should investigate.

- ☐ Who are these people? What goods or services do they need or want? How do they spend their money?
- ☐ What is the present size of the market? What is its anticipated growth?
- ☐ What percentage of the market can you expect to secure with your enterprise?

Look at the businesses in your area. Are there products and services you could provide them? The Employee Assistance Program marketed by Family Services organizations around the country does just this. Local businesses pay Family Services to provide a certain number of counseling hours per month to employees who request it. The corporation saves the cost of adding staff counselors. Family Services earns needed income and better utilizes staff counselors.

4. What you don't have

The preceding sections of this chapter have focused on outlining your assets and opportunities, sketching in broad outline the terrain of enterprise possibilities for your organization.

Now is the time to turn to some of the difficulties, the hurdles to clear before a potential enterprise becomes a real business. This section is designed to help you outline what your organization *doesn't* have in terms of skills, experience, and resources that it will need in order to engage in enterprise. We don't want to label these "organizational deficits" as absolute limits; it's not a case of "you can't get there from here." This section instead should help you identify what capacities or resources your organization needs to develop or acquire in order to proceed along the path toward enterprise.

A. *Capital:*

You need capital to start a business, although different businesses require vastly different amounts of money. Unfortunately, it is the rare nonprofit that has sufficient funds to start an enterprise without borrowing from program funds or endowments. Where can this money be secured? Investors? Bankers? A generous contributor? The truth is that it is *extremely* difficult for any business to raise money and even harder for a nonprofit. List your possible enterprises and then assess each for how much capital would be required to start the business.

B. *Managerial expertise:*

The talents required to run a business are very different from those required to deliver program services. In recent years, however, there has been a growing emphasis on management skills training for nonprofit directors and administrators. However, there may still be a skills gap in your organization when it comes to entrepreneurship.

Who will run the business? What talents and skills are required? Does the enterprise require specific technical know-how to produce products or provide services? What marketing skills are required? Who will identify the distributors and outlets for products, contact suppliers, hire staff? What skills are required to perform those jobs? Is there someone on staff willing and able to devote continuous attention and thorough concentration to this business?

In all honesty, many nonprofits do not have these skills on staff just waiting for an opportunity to be used. The important question to be answered in this section is, Where are they going to come from?

C. *Ancillary services:*

The shift to enterprise will send repercussions of change throughout the organization. Not the least of these changes will be in support services, such as accounting, insurance coverage, personnel policies, and benefits. The changes in themselves are not bad, but an organization should know in advance what changes will occur and how much they will cost.

D. *Tax issues:*

It may be wise to consult your local IRS office to get a determination of whether the revenues from the enterprises under consideration would be ruled as unrelated business income. Some businesses will be clearly one way or the other, but many are ambiguous enough to require IRS review. Because a business will generate unrelated and therefore taxable income is not sufficient reason in itself to eliminate it entirely from consideration. The fact that an enterprise creates taxable income is just one more factor to weigh.

5. *Narrowing the list*

You've mapped out the enterprise terrain and ruled out some areas. Now it is time to begin charting your path by eliminating some of the riskier and less profitable alternatives.

A. *Assets and needs:*

These two factors are the most important in starting a business. The least important factors are what business you have an understanding of or what businesses you would like to be in. If you are like most people, your list of enterprises will probably include one or two enterprises that are personal favorites. Make doubly sure they are real opportunities for the organization.

B. *Think bigger:*

Examine your list of enterprises. How many of them are "street-level" operations—retail outlets, consumer services, etc.? All businesses, big or small, require the same high level of planning, attention, and energy. It takes just as much care to plan and set up a boutique as it does a computer software exchange service.

Don't ignore the enterprise potential in wholesaling. Of the street-level operations on your list, how many could be wholesale enterprises? Remember it's in some sense less difficult to wholesale: You have fewer customers and therefore fewer customer decisions. One customer makes a good start for a software exchange service, but a poor showing for a boutique.

C. *Input/output:*

In starting any business, you want to put the least possible amount in and get the greatest possible amount out. That is, you want to minimize your investment and maximize your return. This goes for skills, assets, money, manpower, time, and attention. Go down your list of enterprise possibilities and examine each of them in these terms. First, eliminate the enterprises that require large capital investments for small returns. Your organization cannot afford such businesses. Those left on the list require less capital to start and maintain and have the possibility of a solid return. However, some businesses in this group can be troublemakers. These are the ones with historically low success rates. They need to be assessed carefully and ruthlessly. If in question about which businesses fit in this category, consult knowledgeable outsiders.[1] Business experts point out that small successes in some cases can be just as costly as big mistakes. It is important to get an accurate forecast of the costs of operation and not to bury costs with program expenses. Also, how much time and attention do these businesses really require day to day? The historical society bookstore, tucked away in some otherwise unusable corner of the lobby, run by volunteers, may require very little staff time and provide a small, steady income. However, closer examination of the real costs may show the shop is actually losing money. The bookstore may not be allocated its share of facilities expenses, or even its equitable share of utility bills. The volunteer sales force is unpaid. Are the paid manager's time and the bookkeeper/accountant's time accurately factored in?

Furthermore, the real costs might be measured more accurately by asking yourself, "What *else* could these volunteers be doing?" Volunteers could perhaps be giving tours of the facility or even of historic buildings or neighborhoods in the city. It is *costing* the nonprofit these services to keep the volunteers tied up in the bookstore. Volunteer time might be leveraged better by examining alternative ways to utilize this resource. When you review your enterprise possibilities, it is crucial to assess these hidden costs.

---

1. For instance, if a bookstore is on your list, check with the American Booksellers Association. They will tell you that fewer than half of their members' stores are profitable.

D. *"Locating" an enterprise:*

In most cases it is best to look for enterprises that share location, markets, or expertise with the parent nonprofit. It's a rule of thumb (for both nonprofits and for-profits) that in acquiring or developing a new enterprise, the leverage for success lies close to home. When you consider it, it's only common sense. Does a farm equipment firm have the experience, expertise, and interest to manage a publishing company successfully? (Although we are not talking about day-to-day management issues, the parent company bears the responsibility for reviewing decisions and options affecting the business; therefore the parent's expertise and experience will be an important factor in the success of the subsidiary.)

The comparative advantage lies close to home where the parent entity, whether nonprofit or profit making, knows the turf, the community, and the people and has the special expertise and experience to contribute to success.

The section entitled "The Spectrum of Nonprofit Enterprise" in chapter 1 outlines some generic nonprofit enterprises and shows their comparative closeness or distance from the parental "home." Review your list of possible enterprises and rank them along this axis according to the distance from the parent nonprofit.

E. *Models:*

Look at what works elsewhere. Do some research and find out what other nonprofits in your community are doing in the way of enterprise. Find out what nonprofits like yours (in size and mission and community environment) are doing in other parts of the country. Try to assess what they have been doing right, and what mistakes they've been making; see what this tells you about your choice. For-profit businesses are also excellent sources of models.

F. *Cooperation and competition:*

Are you setting out to compete with one or more existing for-profits in your community? If so, what is the potential danger that down-the-road charges of unfair competition might be leveled (not without justice) at your enterprise? Is this risk significant or manageable? Is there a way to suggest a cooperative venture instead? Joint ventures (and not only with potential competitors) are avenues to explore, since they are a way of getting someone else to contribute money and/or expertise to leverage your own investment. It is worth the time to look through your list of possibilities and evaluate opportunities for cooperative ventures. Who might be interested in being a partner with your organization in founding this kind of business? If the partner is another nonprofit, what are the pros and cons?

6. The next step

A. If you made it to this point, you probably have a list of several potential enterprises suitable for your organization. But targeting the right enterprise for you and evaluating in detail its chances for success are still ahead. Look through your list of enterprises one final time. Consider each in the light of the following list of the twenty-five most pressing problems for a small business (as identified by the membership of the National Federation of Independent Businesses). This list should help you pinpoint possible problem areas, and might affect your ranking of possible enterprises.

1. Interest rates
2. Cost of insurance
3. Cost of utility bills
4. Cost of labor
5. Local tax rates
6. Locating qualified employees
7. Cost of supplies and inventory
8. Cash flow
9. Low profits
10. Crime rate
11. Competition from large firms
12. Workers' compensation
13. Insufficient sales
14. Controlling inventory
15. Ability to cost-effectively advertise
16. Employee turnover
17. Obtaining needed loans
18. Cost of rent
19. Losing skilled employees to large firms
20. Local inspectors and inspections
21. Obtaining licenses and permits
22. Employee relations and/or unions
23. Unfavorable business location
24. Access to highways, roads, parking, public transportation
25. Garbage collection

B. Develop a detailed business plan for the enterprise you have evaluated as most likely to succeed for your organization. Demonstrating how to design and develop a business plan is beyond the scope of this chapter and study, but the following resources may prove useful:

☐ One excellent sourcebook is *Business Planning Guide*, a handbook on how to develop and use a business plan and financing proposal. The handbook, often distributed through local banks, is also available from Upstart Publishing in Portsmouth, New Hampshire.

☐ The Small Business Administration office in your area has numerous publications to guide you through the process of planning.

☐ Also through the Small Business Administration, you can reach the Active Corps of Executives (ACE) and the Service Corps of Retired Executives (SCORE). Both are organizations of business men and women who donate their time and expertise to others.

☐ Some major metropolitan areas also have other organizations that provide consulting assistance. Certain professional organizations, such as the local chapters of the American Institute of Certified Public Accountants, have committees devoted to community service issues that may be helpful.

7. The last word

Planning is planning, and business is business. No matter how hard or how carefully or even how long you plan, you cannot completely eliminate the risk of a new business through research and reading. Medical textbooks do not make competent doctors, nor do business plans make successful entrepreneurs. You must finally put down the neat business plan and enter the messy marketplace. You may want to take it one small step at a time, beginning with a small business, building and acquiring skills, experience, and confidence before initiating more ambitious enterprises.

chapter 5
RECOMMENDATIONS

he following recommendations are designed to focus attention on ways that various parties—governments, foundations, communities, trustees, staffs, and individuals—can
support enterprise activities in the nonprofit sector. Where
appropriate, these recommendations aim at certain parts of the nonprofit
family and outline specific actions that can be taken. Some of the
recommendations are "lighter" in scope and are designed to have an
immediate impact on situations. Others are "heavier" and have far-
reaching implications that require careful handling, since they seek to
readdress fundamental roadblocks and problems. All the recommendations, in conjunction with the "New Ideas" section that follows, are
aimed at stimulating a new direction of action and enterprise within
the nonprofit community.

A SUMMARY OF THE RECOMMENDATIONS

ORGANIZATION

Recommendation: Focus and highlight the enterprise activity within a nonprofit organization by creating the position "director of enterprise" and finding an individual with entrepreneurial skills to fill it.

CHECKLIST

Recommendation: Create a checklist—one that helps a nonprofit analyze risk factors, competition, and projected profits—for organizations that are interested in becoming involved in enterprise activities.

EVALUATIONS

Recommendation: Set up a standard enterprise reporting process that will help each nonprofit evaluate its enterprise activities and capabilities, and also provide "money sources" with comprehensive information about the nonprofit's activities.

PROFESSIONAL ADVICE

Recommendation: Foundations and the for-profit sector should provide seed money for professional advice (legal, tax, management, marketing, recruiting, and staffing) for nonprofits entering into or enlarging their enterprise activities.

ENTERPRISE GIFTS

Recommendation: Revise corporate giving programs to encourage nonprofit enterprise by making interest-free loans, entering into joint ventures, lending personnel and expertise, and encouraging the use of nonprofit suppliers and subcontractors.

APPROPRIATE MODELS

Recommendation: Provide case studies of successful for-profit businesses, perhaps in workbook form.

CONFERENCES

Recommendation: Organize a national conference where leading nonprofit entrepreneurs can meet and discuss ways of stimulating enterprise activity in the sector. Representatives of grant-making and trustee worlds could participate as observers.

COOPERATION

Recommendation: Nonprofit enterprises should be encouraged to cooperate, rather than compete, with businesses in their communities. Business partnerships with would-be competitors reduce risk, utilize assets, and improve community relations for nonprofit organizations.

EDUCATION

State and local governments:

Recommendation: Conduct a systematic government education program, distributing material to the proper subcommittees and hearings so that governments become more aware of what enterprise can do for the nonprofit sector and learn ways to encourage it.

Trustees:

Recommendation: Draw up a document that spells out what trustees can do to help enterprise in their own institutions, both as individuals and as representatives (which most are) of the for-profit sector. Clarify trustees' understanding of IRS determination of "related" and "unrelated" income.

Staff:

Recommendation: Help staff members accommodate enterprise activities by producing a simple booklet or placing articles in magazines that reach different nonprofit audiences. Staff members should be included in changes; encourage them to cooperate with new people and to help develop new programs.

STATE AND LOCAL GOVERNMENTS

Recommendation: Revise budgetary procedures and other regulations to remove disincentives to institutions that generate income through enterprise activities. Set aside funds to encourage development of nonprofit enterprise.

FURTHER STUDIES

Recommendation: Forego further study of enterprise activities and concentrate time and monies where they will do the most good: developing active programs that help build enterprise in nonprofits.

ORGANIZATION

"To make something happen," the management saying goes, "put someone in charge." This approach works in the nonprofit sector as well. We thus recommend creating a new position, "director of enterprise." The title, obvious as it might seem at first, was chosen with some care. "Director of development" has come to mean fund raising; "director of marketing," although used by some institutions to mean enterprise, usually implies that the person is in charge of marketing the institution; for example, if the institution is a theater, selling tickets. "Director of administration" is an inside title; enterprise is an outside activity. "Director of business development" puts more emphasis on increasing an organization's client base. Enterprise in the nonprofit sector exists to fund its parent institution, not to be a business in and of itself. "Director of enterprise" was chosen to highlight the qualities important to the position: energy, creativity, determination, perseverance. The position calls for an entrepreneur, not a manager or an accountant, who, although qualified to administer and control, may not be entrepreneurial. The true test for the position is the question, Will this person make enterprise happen?

In medium- to large-size nonprofits, we perceive four officers reporting to the president or director of the organization. One is responsible for the institution's program, one for fund raising, one for administration, and one for the ways in which the institution can become more self-supporting through enterprise activities.

Bringing in an entrepreneur or empowering someone to function as an entrepreneur in a nonprofit organization and creating a director-level charter under which that person operates can present problems, however. In the for-profit sector, successful entrepreneurs are well rewarded. In most cases, a nonprofit will have to pay comparably to get comparable talent. Matching profit sector compensation levels may not be necessary if the person is interested in contributing to the nonprofit's overall mission—and is given the opportunity to do so. Some arts organizations and universities have attracted outstanding entrepreneurial help by involving the entrepreneurs in the organization's program, instead of confining their activities solely to filling the treasury.

The director of enterprise may also be paid on an incentive basis.[1] Extraordinary performance may make this person the highest paid member of the staff—even above the president. This situation, which occurs, for example, in sales positions in the for-profit sector, may create problems. Other staff members should be made aware that their benefits, both long and short term, outweigh the liabilities of what may seem like an unfair situation.

1. Although nonprofit status prevents an organization from distributing profits, it can still pay out bonuses, if not incentives per se, linked to sales or profits.

Finding the right person for the position is the most difficult task of all. A desire to devote one's energies to the nonprofit world is not an automatic qualification. Good entrepreneurs are found most readily on the fringes of the for-profit sector, and probably not in large businesses or financial institutions. A board of trustees familiar with the venture capital world may aid the search, as can friends in the for-profit sector who are themselves successful entrepreneurs. Finally, a person may be found who possesses all the qualifications but needs additional training to be really effective. In this case, a short business school stint or a marketing course or two may be a worthwhile investment.

The **recommendation** *is to focus and highlight the enterprise activity within a nonprofit organization by creating the position "director of enterprise" and finding an individual with entrepreneurial strength to fill it.*

It is worth noting that initially fund raisers were outsiders who served as advisers to nonprofit institutions. It was once thought not nice or necessary to solicit funds professionally. But professionals did make a difference, and eventually, fund raising became an indispensable staff function. Today some schools even offer degrees in fund raising and development. If steps are taken now to make a real place for entrepreneurs in the nonprofit world, directors of enterprise may someday be as essential to the funding of a nonprofit organization as fund raisers are today. We certainly hope so.

CHECKLIST

Many of the businesses that are easy to get into are also easy to get out of. Enterprises with traditionally high failure rates—boutiques, restaurants, bakeries, publishing ventures—are the very enterprises to which nonprofits are most often attracted. The American Booksellers Association reports that 50 percent of its member bookstores lose money. The restaurant world experiences a tremendous turnover, and the rate of bankruptcy among gifts shops is high. Businesses that seem accessible because we have all had *customer* experience with them are difficult to run and even tougher to make turn a profit. They also consume a great deal of capital before a single sale is made.

A simple checklist—one that helps a nonprofit analyze risk factors, competition, and projected profits—would be useful to organizations interested in becoming involved in such ventures. If the results point toward going forward, then institutions can take the next step and write a business plan.

Although many of the businesses that attract nonprofits seem to require little capital, talent, and know-how to start, they also have little leverage, scale, or market position once they get going. A "pre-flight checklist" would help a nonprofit entering such an enterprise maximize its competitive advantage and use whatever leverage it has. It might also lead an organization to decide that the risk and work are not worth the projected profits. The checklist is something against which each institution can test its judgment.

The **recommendation** *is to create a checklist for business possibilities in the nonprofit sector that will help allay surprise, failure, and false hopes.*

EVALUATIONS

Foundations and other funding sources that evaluate the fiscal health of nonprofit organizations need a reliable system for determining the extent and success of each nonprofit's enterprise activities. Although the larger institutions keep comprehensive books, the majority of non-profits (even though they produce solid financial statements) tend to lump enterprise activities with other earned revenue streams. A more detailed accounting of various streams would help nonprofits evaluate the success of their enterprises and would also provide those organizations with the means to evaluate the success of various enterprise ventures.

A conference of representatives of the major auditing firms that deal with nonprofits might help set up standard evaluation methods. In addition, if grantors demand better accounting for enterprise ventures and make this a condition of grant participation, nonprofits will learn quickly how to report their activities to the benefit of both grantors and the organization.

The **recommendation** *is to host a conference of involved auditors to set up a standardized enterprise reporting process to help nonprofits evaluate their enterprise activities and capabilities. This conference could also provide grant-makers with comprehensive information about a nonprofit's self-help activities.*

PROFESSIONAL ADVICE

Nonprofit organizations entering into or enlarging their enterprise operations usually need substantial advice on legal matters, taxes, man-agement, marketing, recruiting, and staffing. Unfortunately, profes-sional advice costs money, which is hard to part with, especially when the institution's necessary programs are already strapped for funds. The irony is that at the very moment it has a low priority, such advice is probably most needed.

Foundations, trustees, and corporations can (1) supply funds for needed professional consultants and thus provide leverage and/or (2) lend the advice of their own professional staffs. Whatever the tactic, sound professional advice must find its way into the nonprofit sector. Enterprise activity often grows in an ad hoc fashion within nonprofit institutions. If it is to make a meaningful contribution to these organizations, professional guidance from other sources must be supplied.

The recommendation is that foundations and the for-profit sector provide seed money for professional advice or actually provide the talent. Such advice would help create successful enterprise models for other nonprofit organizations.

ENTERPRISE GIFTS

It would seem that corporations that understand enterprise, know how to help, and know where and when help is needed should consider a new kind of giving to the nonprofit sector. Most corporate foundations are stretched to the limits of their capacity to be good citizens in every community where they have a presence. But a corporation can donate in other ways. It can give advice, lend personnel, and encourage the use of nonprofits as suppliers and subcontractors. It can also combine in joint ventures and lend its cash flow. The latter can benefit nonprofit enterprises that need working capital. Such a loan could be set up as a regular business loan, except that the corporation could forego interest, deducting the interest it might have earned as a contribution. The loan, of course, would have to be paid back. Should the venture fail, the loan could still be considered a contribution. The objective, however, is to pay the corporation back.

With interest rates fluctuating between 15 and 20 percent, however, many corporations simply don't have the cash to lend. Companies seeking to help more institutions might consider converting some of their donations to enterprise loans, some of which would eventually be repaid.

The recommendation is to promote enterprise giving by corporations as an alternative to systems based solely on donations. Such an alternative would permit corporations to be more helpful to nonprofits and to use their skills where they can do the most good. Although cash-flow loans should be investigated, the for-profit sector can offer people, expertise, and connections most readily. Many national corporate entities can operate as joint venture partners, advisers, or sources of occasional help at crucial junctures where and when specific talents and experience are needed. These assets should be offered, and nonprofits should not hesitate to ask for such assistance.

APPROPRIATE MODELS

Nonprofit enterprises tend to be small and need a level of management appropriate to their size. They shouldn't be run ad hoc, but neither should they be strangled with too many controls. Too much accounting, too much planning, too many of the trappings of big business or business schools can be just as detrimental to such organizations as too little guidance. Somewhere between the overly casual business practices of many nonprofits and the elaborate control systems of big business lies an appropriate middle ground where the real costs and profits of each nonprofit enterprise can be calculated and understood.

Successful, small for-profit businesses provide good models for nonprofit enterprise to study and at times copy. Case studies of for-profit small businesses should be encouraged in business schools as well as in the nonprofit sector. Similarly, nonprofits should identify and seek out successful for-profit entrepreneurs for information and advice about running small enterprises.

The **recommendation** *is to encourage and aid the development of an appropriate "board of experts" for small enterprises within the nonprofit sector and to entice business schools and others to provide necessary data or produce a series of usable small-business case studies.*

CONFERENCES

In the past few years, dozens of conferences have explored various aspects of nonprofit enterprise. Most have given those considering enterprise a chance to hear from those who are actually doing it. Although these conferences are helpful, we believe it would also be advantageous to bring together leading entrepreneurs from all areas of the nonprofit sector, to give them a chance to share their experiences and learn from each other. Such a conference would set up a forum for an exchange of ideas and strategies for building nonprofit enterprise in the future. In addition, it might provide the basis for an informal network whereby successful nonprofit entrepreneurs can move from smaller institutions to larger ones, much in the same way that their counterparts in the for-profit sector move through various sizes of business organizations.

The **recommendation** *is to organize a national conference where leading non-profit entrepreneurs can meet and discuss ways of infusing enterprise activities into the sector. Representatives of the grant-making and trustee worlds would also be encouraged to participate—as observers—but the floor would belong to the entrepreneurs and their needs and concerns.*

COOPERATION

Many nonprofits choose to compete (or end up competing) with for-profit small businesses in their own communities. They are often not even aware of this situation until a lawyer pays them a visit or the town council questions their tax-exempt status. Most of the conflicts involving nonprofit enterprise have stemmed from a for-profit entity crying "unfair." In some instances, nonprofits have wisely retreated; others have stood their ground; and still others have worked out some accommodation with the profit-making entity.

The problem, however, can largely be avoided by simple observation: Are there similar enterprises in the area that are likely to be affected by competition from a nonprofit organization? If so, the nonprofit might consider cooperation instead of competition. Specifically, nonprofits should look to the for-profit sector for business partners. If a nonprofit organization has spare facilities, such as printing equipment, dining areas, or computers, it might set up a partnership with a local printer, caterer, or computer service house to use these assets. Veterans in a particular business usually know far better than novices where to look for customers and pitfalls. Reinventing the wheel is inefficient in any field, and riskier in a small business where the market may already be fully penetrated.

As a case in point, consider a university that uses its kitchen downtime to go into the catering business. With its large capacity, it begins to compete successfully with existing catering businesses in the community. The university's success, however, might make it difficult for some for-profit caterers to survive, thus increasing the demands on the university kitchens to supply the community's needs. The university then might have to make additional investments in equipment and staff to continue to service the needs of the community—whether or not it really wants to be in the catering business. The long-term disservice done to the community and the university itself might outweigh the short-run benefits of the university's use of facilities downtime.

A better alternative might be for the university to make its facilities available to local caterers in return for their expertise; such a partnership could reduce risk, increase profits, and improve relations with the community. If local businesses are disinclined to join, then at least the nonprofit has tried. If businesses do want to cooperate, they can take on many of the managerial and administrative headaches that are essential to that business. The nonprofit gets the benefit of proven management when it creates such a joint venture.

Most trustees come from the community's bigger businesses and may not be aware of the problem of grassroots competition. But once informed, they must be able to help the nonprofit find business partners, who, in common cause with the nonprofit, can help it survive. Local business might want to help in this way. It certainly makes more sense than engaging their ire and risking the consequences in the courts that might follow.

The recommendation is for nonprofit enterprises to cooperate, rather than compete, with businesses in their communities. Business partnerships with would-be competitors reduce risk, utilize assets, and improve community relations for nonprofit organizations as well as provide experienced management.

EDUCATION

Enterprise fails to develop in many nonprofit institutions or communities largely because those involved don't know how to encourage it or don't understand the contribution it can make to nonprofits. In short, education is desperately needed.

State and Local Governments

Particularly now, when state and local governments must cut back aid to literally thousands of institutions, legislators and bureaucrats need to know the advantages of encouraging nonprofit self-sufficiency and of creating a more supportive climate for nonprofit enterprise. In particular, the procedures and attitudes that penalize nonprofits that generate at least part of their income should be reexamined. This and other related topics are discussed in depth in the section "State and Local Government" in this chapter.

The recommendation is to conduct a systematic government education program, distributing material to the proper subcommittees and hearings so that governments become more aware of what enterprise can do and learn how to encourage it.

Trustees

In order to be receptive to enterprise activity in nonprofit institutions, trustees need a clear understanding of how the IRS determines "related" and "unrelated" business income. A rethinking of long-held prejudices against nonprofits' paying taxes is also important—as we pointed out earlier in this report, organizations should not deprive themselves of economic self-sufficiency simply because earning income means dealing with the IRS.

Trustees also need to know how enterprise works in the nonprofit sector, the difference it makes, and how other organizations are being helped by it. Last, but far from least, they need to know how they can help—how their particular expertise and knowledge can be useful in putting together a successful enterprise activity for their organization.

*The **recommendation** is to draw up a document that spells out what trustees can do to help enterprise in their own institutions—both as individuals and as representatives, which many are, of the for-profit sector.*

Staffs

Staff members should not feel that they are "selling out" or "being sold out" if their institution engages in enterprise activities. It doesn't mean they have to shed their habits and values; it simply means that the institution has a new source of support. They should be included in the process and encouraged to work with the new people in their midst and to help develop new ideas.

*The **recommendation** is to report on how institutions deal with this change, how programs benefit, and how staffs accommodate enterprise, either by producing a simple booklet or placing articles in magazines that reach different nonprofit audiences.*

Education should help remove misgivings and roadblocks to enterprise. Speeches, articles, and pamphlets will go a long way in correcting misconceptions and gaining support for enterprise in the nonprofit sector.

STATE AND LOCAL GOVERNMENTS

As we pointed out in the "Education" section, state legislators and bureaucrats need to be educated on the advantages of creating a more supportive climate for nonprofit enterprise.[2] At present, nonprofit organizations in numerous states are penalized for their enterprise activities. The more self-supporting they are, the less they are eligible for state aid. Although these policies protect institutions with no other means of support, they also encourage nonprofits in general to maximize their need, rather than their self-sufficiency.

*The **recommendation** is to revise budgetary procedures so as to remove penalties to institutions that generate income through enterprise activities. In addition, we recommend shifting some government funds into a special category to help nonprofits initiate enterprise activities. In the long run, this approach would save both the government and the taxpayers money and*

---

2. Specifically, state legislatures might consider requiring insurance companies that do business in the state to reimburse for services provided by qualified nonprofit programs. The counseling programs of mental health or drug rehabilitation programs could qualify for the same insurance reimbursements as do private practitioners (M.D.'s and Ph.D.'s). This policy would allow nonprofits providing such services to expand their clientele and increase their earned income.

would make more government aid available to those institutions that have no capacity for self-support.

FURTHER STUDIES

Those of us who worked on this study worried about the quantity and quality of the data available. But as our familiarity with the subject grew, we realized that the study of enterprise is institution-specific and most useful in that form. The conclusions and generalizations we made from the hard data collected have served as useful jumping-off points. But the fragmentation within the sector makes collecting more hard data prohibitively expensive and probably not worth the cost.

What nonprofit enterprise *does* need is help in gaining expertise, raising working capital, documenting successful models for others to emulate, attracting entrepreneurs to the sector, and finding and developing the ones that are already there. The problem lies with the tools of entrepreneurship—money and managers—not the data. Numbers and studies don't build successful enterprises; money, people, products, and services do.

A longitudinal study of select enterprise operations, based on standardized reporting, might help; so might funding to focus attention on developing systematic accounting standards and reporting models. But, barring these, what are most useful are not more studies but more active programs that work alongside emerging enterprises, helping them grow.

*The **recommendation** is to forego further study of enterprise activities and concentrate time and monies where they will do the most good: on developing active programs that help build enterprise in the nonprofit sector.*

chapter 6
NEW IDEAS

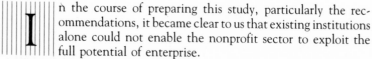 n the course of preparing this study, particularly the recommendations, it became clear to us that existing institutions alone could not enable the nonprofit sector to exploit the full potential of enterprise.

The gray areas where sectors overlap, where the regulations concerning tax and legal status are confusing, must be cleared up before nonprofit enterprise can achieve its real growth potential. What is needed is a "hunting license" for the sector to engage in enterprise, with restrictions spelled out straightforwardly and consistently for all inside and outside the sector to see. In lieu of hoping to wake up one morning to find that federal, state, and local governments have established clear and consistent policy guidelines on the subject, the sector must move on its own behalf, not just to recommend changes, but to see they are put into effect.

Ideally, some flagship institution in the sector might push this initiative. In reality, it is beyond the scope and resources of any single nonprofit to undertake this task. Neither should any individual institution be expected to put itself and its programs at risk for a cause that will benefit the whole sector.

A cooperative effort among nonprofits is another possible but unlikely solution. Nonprofits have a poor record of collaboration, in part because it is more difficult for nonprofits to share. In profit sector collaborations, the division of investment and income is relatively easy: It is a matter of dollars and cents. In the nonprofit sector, a whole range of non-quantifiables enter the formula—pride, mission, responsibility, prestige, service—and make division an almost impossible task. In addition, there are no mechanisms to ease the way for cooperation, to mediate misunderstanding, and to clarify the confusion inevitable in any cooperative venture.

Beyond a clear license to engage in enterprise, the sector will also require a level of working capital and expertise not yet available. A single organization may be able to raise the funds and secure the talent to take on an ambitious enterprise, but it will have no carryover benefit for the sector. The sector needs a pool of entrepreneurial talent and a career path for these entrepreneurs to follow. Single nonprofits and their enterprises simply cannot provide this.

To create the greatest possible opportunities for enterprise in the sector, we propose the following institutional-level innovations:

A NEW ENTITY

We first propose for further study a new kind of nonprofit entity, which we call a 501(c)(3)x. The 501(c)(3)x would give qualifying nonprofits a clear "license" for enterprise. At the same time, it would ensure that enterprising nonprofits continue to validate their mission through community support. Basically, to qualify for the 501(c)(3)x a nonprofit would have to raise at least 20 percent of its revenues from the community. Up to 80 percent of operating funds could come from enterprise, but no more. In this way, the more successful a nonprofit's enterprise activities became, the more rigorously it would have to continue to demonstrate its ability to attract funding from its community.

The 501(c)(3)x, as we see it, would be permitted to earn unrelated business income, but it would file a tax form on such income, comparable to forms for for-profit companies. However, rather than turning over the assessed taxes to the IRS or state tax agencies, it would have to designate that amount to its parent for program-related expenses. It could not reinvest these "taxes" in the enterprise. We feel this provision would go a long way to eliminate the growing cries of unfair competition from for-profit counterparts. Nonprofit enterprises have found themselves recently in rancorous disputes with small local businesses in competition for the same market. And the cries of "unfair" admittedly have merit. A small businessman may not object to supporting a local nonprofit passively through his taxes, but if the same nonprofit goes into direct competition with him, his charitable instincts may be strained to the breaking point.

With a 501(c)(3)x provision, enterprising nonprofits could compete on an equal footing. The market would determine the rest. The for-profit business's taxes would go to the government while the 501(c)(3)x's "taxes" would go directly to delivering needed services in the community, bypassing the distributive bureaucracies. (It is worth noting that this self-payment system efficiently delivers needed funds to valued programs while helping reduce bureaucracies because it eliminates the lengthy governmental funds allocation processes.) At the same time, because 501(c)(3)x's must raise 20 percent of their income from contributions, the community is assured that nonprofits will continue to deliver the services it needs and wants.

COOPERATIVE ENTERPRISES

Past attempts to encourage cooperation among nonprofits have tended to *push*—to force shotgun marriages for survival's sake, without regard for resistance and bruised self-images. We believe that significant benefits can be gained from increased cooperation among nonprofits and that the poor record of the past can be improved by *pulling* nonprofits toward cooperation, by providing mechanisms to draw individual units into loose associations with the promise of greater opportunities. Therefore, we offer for consideration the following businesses, which we believe can generate self-supporting revenue and simultaneously serve the sector.

Merchandising

Many nonprofits already run successful enterprises on a local or regional scale and could profit from expanding their markets. We propose the creation of a mail-order catalog business that could offer the products of nonprofit enterprises to customers nationwide. A catalog, perhaps like the successful Horchow Collection catalog, could merchandise these products attractively. The company could be much more than a simple listing service; once on a solid footing, it could provide financing for expansion and consultation on manufacture and merchandising.

To be included in the catalog, every item would be subject to review, primarily for quality control. (The good name of the catalog company and of every nonprofit appearing in it would be at stake.) After careful review, the company would then place an initial order for goods with the nonprofit, which, if necessary, would then use those funds to tool up to the required level and quality of production. The catalog company will profit by taking the usual retail percentage of the purchase. The nonprofit will profit by gaining a nationwide clientele. Lists for mailing would be purchased from nonprofits around the country. Department stores and other retailers would be encouraged to donate their lists and take a tax deduction. (It may prove to be more efficient to package the catalog operation for an existing catalog company to run. In that case, a small project team might be assigned to organize and oversee the manufacturing end of the operation, to guide nonprofits, and to review items for possible inclusion.)

If the catalog proved successful, the company might explore the possibility of opening a catalog store in selected locations. Using the same products, the same review process, and the same advance order system as the catalog operation, a nonprofit boutique, located in a downtown shopping area or suburban mall with heavy pedestrian traffic, might be a profitable second outlet for items produced or licensed by nonprofits.

Exchange Clearinghouse

Many nonprofits, especially the smaller ones, have found trading or barter to be one effective way of stretching limited dollars. We propose that a nonprofit enterprise be established to develop opportunities for exchange. A number of companies organized regionally could act as clearinghouses for nonprofits in their areas. Each company would regularly publish an inexpensive newspaper listing (e.g., in a neighborhood classified paper) of exchange opportunities for nonprofits in the region. Organizations could list their available surpluses and needed goods and services. The clearinghouse company would charge a membership fee and a small fee for every listing. It could also act as a barter "bank." Member nonprofits could then build up debits and credits, so that barter transactions could involve several nonprofit organizations and/or be spread over a period of time.

For instance, a dance company looking for studio space and a symphony looking for transportation might both be able to barter for those commodities with a private school in their area, using the downtime of its gymnasium and buses. The school would build up a certain number of exchange credits for the transaction. Or, the clearinghouse might arrange for the dancers and symphony to "pay" the school for these services with performances or lessons for students.

Product Development

Because many individual nonprofits have developed goods and services of potential use to others in the sector, we propose a nonprofit company be formed to develop and market these products. One nonprofit, for instance, has developed computer software for its accounting needs. This software could be developed into a generic package for use throughout the sector. The development company would invest in refining the software and then market it to other nonprofits. Revenues from the sale of the product would be divided between the originator and the development company.

THE NON-PROFIT ENTERPRISE DEVELOPMENT CORPORATION

To create a pool of venture capital (without competing with other nonprofits for the same limited funds) and to develop a bank of managerial expertise, we propose that a venture capital firm (along the lines of those in the for-profit sector) be created for nonprofit enterprises. This firm, which we have called the Non-Profit Enterprise Development Corporation (NPEDC), could be set up as a 501(c)(3) with the mission of providing the necessary means (capital and expertise) to assist nonprofit organizations in fostering enterprise.

We believe that such a venture investment entity could go a long way toward providing the working capital and expertise necessary to raise the level of enterprise opportunity in the sector.

The NPEDC would be modeled on profit sector venture capital firms. Nonprofit applicants for investment would submit a detailed business plan of proposed enterprises according to guidelines and procedures established by NPEDC. The staff would review the plan and make recommendations to the board. The board, composed of men and women with experience in for-profit venture firms and those with experience and expertise in the special problems of the nonprofit sector, would make the final decision on the application and the amount to be invested.

As in for-profit venture firms, the investment would take the form not just of capital but of expertise. The staff of the firm, drawing on a range of managerial and technical experience, would closely follow funded enterprises and provide guidance. This staff expertise is necessary to run any profitable venture capital firm. But, it will also benefit the whole sector. Indeed, we would suggest that NPEDC offer its expertise to the companies in which it invests and also on a fee-for-service basis at fair market prices to any nonprofit enterprise. In the long run, we believe that through its venture investments and consulting, NPEDC could be instrumental in attracting top-quality managerial talent to the sector, talent that might otherwise remain in for-profit organizations.

We strongly believe, based on the findings of our report, that if such a venture capital firm were to be established, it should be unequivocally dedicated to aiding *enterprise* in the nonprofit sector, *not* simply to aiding the nonprofit sector. Its intent should be to make money for the sector, not to do good. There is a critical difference. It should not shelter the enterprises of nonprofits from the real world of business, but aid them in rising to its challenges. The venture capital firm should be free to identify and fund successful enterprises without getting a black eye. It should not be designed to distribute money for programs, no matter how worthy. It should not be a fund for program-related investments or the creation of model programs, which have proved to be of limited value and profitability in the past. Rather, we believe that this venture capital entity should be clearly set up as a business that invests in other businesses (all founded by nonprofits).

With a relatively modest amount of seed capital, we believe that the NPEDC framework could be set up. A venture pool could then be raised from corporations and foundations. By investing in the fund, foundations would multiply the value of their grant or gift many times over, not just for the grantee institution but for the whole sector. Corporate donors might also supply initial funds as long-term loans without interest. They would be able to deduct the amount of forgone interest as a contribution. Eventually, the venture capital firm would pay back the initial loans, and the pool would sustain itself through profits on its investments.

THE NPEDC ENTERPRISE CORPS

As important as raising working capital to fund nonprofit enterprises is the need to attract managerial talent to run them. Young men and women who choose careers in the nonprofit sector do so for reasons very different from those who choose to start or manage businesses. In all fairness, there are few opportunities for ambitious young business school graduates to make their mark in the nonprofit sector. By creating more enterprise opportunities, more talented managers will be drawn to the sector. But in addition to attracting talent, it will be necessary to develop managers with expertise in the special problems of nonprofit enterprises and to provide career paths.

To develop business, financial, managerial, and technical expertise in the nonprofit sector, we propose the creation of a program for business school students and recent graduates to serve internships in nonprofit organizations. The goal of this program, which we would call the Enterprise Corps, is twofold: in the short run, to provide top-quality business talent for the sector to put to use in enterprise growth; and in the long run, to attract more trained business professionals to the sector.

Interns could be assigned to the NPEDC in the venture capital firm. From there, they could be rotated to field assignments as consultants to nonprofits that are developing business plans for future enterprises or to new ventures in the critical start-up stage.

Participants in the Enterprise Corps would be chosen competitively and paid salaries commensurate with their counterparts in the for-profit sector. The cost of the program might be paid by corporate sponsors (much like an extension of an executive loan program). Or, the NPEDC could carry the cost of the program as a legitimate expense. The interns will contribute, after all, to its profitability with their expertise.

EPILOGUE

he report is finished. The typewriters are quiet. We have shared our findings and our thoughts on the promise of enterprise. Yet we feel this report should end on a cautionary note.

Cash-hungry nonprofits turn toward each new source of funding relief like cattle toward a watering hole, looking for sustenance and survival. Enterprise, unfortunately, is no such oasis. Grant requests or fund appeals are answered—affirmative or negative—in a short period. The organization risks only paper and time. If the answer is no, it is relatively easy to write off the effort and get in the next grant race or start a new fund drive.

Enterprise is a far different matter. It is a distance event, not a sprint. One must risk money and management time and expertise and even lost opportunities, and still there are no guarantees. Even if one achieves positive results—profits—they may disappear for reasons beyond one's control. The game is not easy. Today's success can easily become tomorrow's failure. Enterprise requires perseverance and a dedication to rethinking and reworking each twist in the chain of events. It requires a special kind of leadership and outlook, a willingness to take risks. It is a journey into new territory with only the sketchiest of maps. Entrepreneurs need to listen, adapt, and scramble. Perhaps the last requirement—scrambling—is the most important.

Entrepreneurs in the for-profit sector occur in about one out of fifty individuals at best. Our evidence in the nonprofit sector suggests they occur only in one out of perhaps two hundred.

There are many nonprofit directors who are gifted leaders and managers, but who may not be equally skilled at fund raising. There is no reason to expect that scholars, social workers, or performers have the skills and motivation to be winning fund raisers. Nonprofits have often solved this problem by hiring a fund raiser (or director of development). The same approach should be considered for enterprise activities. But whether one identifies an entrepreneur inside the organization or brings one in from outside, the problem is far from solved. It takes time to choose the right enterprise—one that could generate an acceptable return on investment and that keeps the organizational risk at a manageable level.

The bottom line is that enterprise takes time. Enterprise revenues can make an important contribution. However, enterprise is not an instant answer, and the odds of losing are greater than those of winning. Most new small businesses fail within the first two years. Success requires careful planning, hard work, unrelenting attention to detail, and a little luck.

The good news is that some nonprofit businesses, particularly those that are close to home, *are* doing well. These often survive because the community views the enterprise as another way to give to the institution and to get something in return. Although these contribution-type enterprises usually work initially, their growth is limited. The name of the institution is often more important than the product or service itself. The market, in short, is limited to those to whom the name means something worth supporting. Still, this may be one of the best ways to grow larger enterprises.

As one moves further from home, the risks increase. Managing unfamiliar enterprises is dangerous at best. Conglomerates that try it often fail. There is reason to believe that small nonprofits will not fare any better.

A stampede of anxious nonprofits to enterprise would probably endanger important programs and even hasten the demise of some organizations. Enterprise is a road that must be traveled cautiously.

This final, sober caveat is meant only to remove false hopes, not to dampen spirits.

Over the past six months, we have spoken to many men and women and heard of many more who have made enterprise happen. We thank them; their examples instruct us all and give us reason and inspiration to proceed. Enterprise is alive and well. It is helping many nonprofits, and it can and will help others.

APPENDIXES

Appendix A

STUDY METHODOLOGY

Defining Our Data Base

The nonprofit sector encompasses a broad range of types of tax-exempt organizations [as determined by Internal Revenue Code section 501(a)] established to meet a variety of needs and objectives. In the *Yale Law Journal* (April 1980), Henry R. Hansmann, professor of law at the University of Pennsylvania, provides a straightforward definition: "A nonprofit organization is, in essence, an organization that is barred from distributing its net earnings, if any, to individuals who exercise control over it, such as members, officers, directors, or trustees." Nonprofits are regulated by what he calls the "nondistribution constraint." We have narrowed our field of interest principally to those nonprofits that have tax-exempt status under the Internal Revenue Code 501(c)(3).[1] Section 501(c)(3) is the only category [under section 501(a)] that "automatically qualifies donors for charitable contribution deductions."

We have also drawn some examples of enterprise from the cooperative sector. These are not 501(c)(3) organizations. Hansmann explains the difference: "Cooperatives are generally formed under state cooperative corporation statutes and the business corporation statutes. Cooperative corporation statutes typically permit a cooperative's net earnings to be distributed to its patrons or investors, who may in turn exercise control over the organization. Thus cooperatives are not subject to the nondistribution constraint that is the definitive characteristic of nonprofit organizations." Despite this distinction, we found several cooperatives that provided useful examples of enterprise, including several cooperatives composed of 501(c)(3) organizations. Two major categories of 501(c)(3) organizations that we excluded as not germane to the objectives of our study were hospitals and religiously affiliated organizations.

Once we determined our broad objectives, several methods were used to gather information. Since one primary objective was to obtain firsthand information from a diverse group of 501(c)(3)'s, we attempted to seek a broad base in terms of the following:

☐ Mission/purpose
☐ Geographical location
  • All regions of the country
  • Major metropolitan areas, other cities and towns, and rural areas

---

1. According to the IRS, organizations classified as 501(c)(3) are those "operated exclusively for religious, charitable, scientific, testing for public safety, literary or educational purposes or for the prevention of cruelty to children or animals (includes hospitals, churches and schools or organizations which foster international amateur sports competition)."

☐ Size—budget, revenues, and staff
☐ Age
☐ Management attitudes

The following chart provides an alphabetical listing of the different types of nonprofits from which information was gathered. These types fall under the major headings "arts" and "human services," although a number are hybrids; others have education as a primary or secondary mission.

TYPES OF ORGANIZATIONS INVESTIGATED

Organization	Arts/ Human Services	Audience/ Client
Aging	HS	Client
Arts centers	A	Aud
Botanical gardens, arboretums	A	Aud
Camps	HS	Client
Child welfare	HS	Client
Community development	HS	Client
Criminal justice, prison reform	HS	Client
Environmental, nature centers, energy	HS	Client
Family services—counseling, crisis intervention	HS	Client
Handicapped—physically, emotionally, mentally	HS	Client
Historical society, preservation	A	Aud
Libraries	A	Aud
Media arts—film, video	A	Aud
Mental health	HS	Client
Museums—art, natural history, science & technology, planetarium	A	Aud
Opera companies	A	Aud
Private secondary school (nonsectarian)	HS	Client
Research organizations	HS	Client
Substance abuse—drug, alcohol	HS	Client
Symphony orchestras	A	Aud
Theater	A	Aud
Universities/colleges	HS	Client
Zoos/aquariums	A	Aud

We also categorized these organizations on the basis of people served. Some organizations serve an audience—people who seek out the organization's program for entertainment, education, or another form of leisure-time activity. These groups have the ability (although some may be prohibited by charter) to charge an *admission fee*. Zoos, museums, and theaters are examples. Other groups serve clients—people who seek out the organization's services or programs for some form of help, counseling, consulting, or education. These groups have the ability to charge a *fee for service*. The chart shows which types fall into which categories.

To determine our specific targets, we took several approaches simultaneously. One was to find the "watering hole" for each major type of organization—that is, to what associations or entities does an organization turn for professional support and assistance? We contacted the umbrella organizations that represent museums, opera companies, agencies serving the blind, college and university business officers, and many others; we eventually reached more than twenty-five associations. In each case, we explained the purpose of the study and enlisted their assistance in contacting nonprofits. We purchased or received free membership lists from many. Most associations were helpful and interested in the data we were collecting. Some were able to provide excellent leads.

A second source was the telephone Yellow Pages. To ensure geographical diversity, we selected eighteen metropolitan areas and prepared lists of nonprofits in those areas using the Yellow Pages' system of indexing. Federal government offices, foundations, and corporations also provided information about organizations that might be of interest to this report.

The second broad objective of the study was that we wanted our methodology to provide a good "listening post" to the organizations we found so that we would learn as much as possible from them. Data collection relied on the use of an exhaustive questionnaire, extensive telephone interviews, and following up on leads.

Our questionnaire was sent to 1,800 nonprofit organizations across the country, including an explanatory cover letter and a business reply envelope. We determined our mailing lists from the membership directories discussed previously and from specific leads and referrals. Our response was under 10 percent, which was disappointing. The questionnaire's comprehensiveness no doubt contributed to the low response rate. Every subject covered was designed to yield useful information about the organization—how it is managed fiscally and administratively; what its management's attitude is toward "enterprise." We also designed the questionnaire to be useful to the responding organization. For instance, section E, which provided a "laundry list" of possible entrepreneurial activities for nonprofits, might give some new ideas to a nonprofit organization's executives.

Although the *quantity* of the responses was disappointing, the *quality*, in general, was impressive. Most respondents were generous and complete with their answers and with the supporting information they provided. Most responses indicated a concern about how their organization was presented and a high level of interest in the study's results. Everyone completing a questionnaire requested a copy of the report.

We learned that timing can dramatically affect response rate, depending on the organization's internal schedule and workload when the questionnaire is received. For example, because of their performance schedule, fall is the worst time for an orchestra management staff to answer a questionnaire. We learned that many organizations have been barraged with requests to complete forms. They range from studies by government entities, to funding sources, to Ph.D. candidates' theses, to professional associations.

We received several letters expressing regret for not having time to complete the survey. A few responses were antagonistic; one said that since we received the funding and his organization did not, he declined to participate. Some respondents wanted reassurance about the origin of the study and its potential audience and use; upon being contacted with an explanation, they readily provided information.

Other than the questionnaire, telephone interviews proved to be an exceptionally rich source of information. All examples used in the report are based on extensive phone interviews, an analysis of completed questionnaires, annual reports, and other written material—or a combination of techniques.

Finally, we asked permission to use quotes and to refer to organizations specifically. We trust we have honored all requests to maintain the anonymity of sources who did not wish to be named.

Appendix B

DATA SUMMARY

General Comments

The following analyses are based on the responses from the questionnaire we sent to approximately 1,800 nonprofits around the country. Several points should be kept in mind in reviewing the findings:

☐ The response rate was under 10 percent, and the following findings must be viewed in the light of the size of the sample.

☐ Within each category, the data base size may change because of availability of raw data on any particular subject.

☐ Further data collection and analysis would be required to reach definitive conclusions. The presentation of this analysis is intended to show trends and patterns only.

Sample Distribution

The respondents to our questionnaires represent a diverse range of nonprofits in terms of their geographical location, budget, and staff sizes. Tables B-1, B-2, and B-3 show the distribution of responses. As discussed in the introduction to the study, we intentionally focused on small- and middle-size organizations, not the so-called "Fortune 500" of the nonprofit sector.

Table B-1.

BUDGET SIZE OF RESPONDENTS

Budget Size ($000)	Percentage of Respondents	
0–100	14	
101–300	32	
301–600	9	49%
601–800	5	in 100–1,000
801–1000	3	range
1,001–1,500	9	
1,501–4,000	15	
4,001–10,000	7	
10,001 and above	6	
	100	

Table B-2.

STAFF SIZE OF RESPONDENTS

Full-Time Staff Size	Percentage of Respondents	
0–5	32	63%
6–10	15	have 20 or
11–20	16	fewer full-time
21–100	20	employees
101 and up	17	
	100	

Table B-3.

SOURCE OF SAMPLE BY SIZE OF POPULATION CENTER

1980 Population Density	Location of U.S. Population (%)	Location of Sample (%)
Small (fewer than 250,000 people)	38	42
Medium (250,000–999,999)	23	29
Large (1,000,000 and up)	39	29
	100	100

Enterprise Comparisons

General

The following observations can be made from an overall look at our data:

☐ Of the sample for which information on enterprise activities was produced, over 60 percent generate *some* of their revenues from these activities.

☐ Of the sample involved in enterprise, over the five-year period for which data were provided, enterprise revenues as a percentage of total *expanded* in over 60 percent of the groups and *contracted* in less than 25 percent.

☐ For our total sample, *average budget growth* from 1976 to 1981 was 139 percent, and 64 percent experienced *real* budget growth (in excess of inflation).

☐ For organizations that saw enterprise revenues become a more significant share of their income, the budgets grew on average over 200 percent.

☐ For those groups for which enterprise comprised a smaller percentage of total income in 1981 than in 1976, the average budget grew only 106 percent.

☐ In summary, although this information is in no way conclusive, it does indicate that enterprise revenues represent an attitude that reflects itself in terms of dynamism, growth, and vitality.

Budget size versus enterprise

Table B-4 compares budget and staff size to enterprise revenues. The average staff size of our sample is given for each budget size range, although staff size varies greatly depending on many independent and organization-specific factors.

Table B-4.

BUDGET SIZE VERSUS ENTERPRISE "REVENUES"

Average Staff Size	1981 Budget Size ($000)	Enterprise Revenues as a Percentage of Total Revenue					
		0%	1–1.99%	2–4.99%	5–9.99%	10% or more	*Total*
2	0–100	63	6	19	6	6	100
7	101–300	48	11	9	7	25	100
12	301–600	60	20	—	—	20	100
22	601–1,000	38	25	—	25	12	100
43	1,001–1,500	63	12	—	—	25	100
87	1,501–4,000	12	25	25	13	25	100
144	4,001–10,000	44	—	14	14	28	100
355	10,001 and above	—	17	51	16	16	100

A number of interesting observations can be made from these data:

☐ Overall, about 40 percent of the relevant sample generate *none* of their revenues from what we call "enterprise activities."

☐ The very small organizations (budget size under $100,000) in general do not rely on enterprise revenues.

☐ Of the sample with budgets over $10 million, all have some amount of enterprise.

☐ Organizations that rely to a significant degree (10 percent or more of their total revenues) on enterprise activities do not fall into any particular size category. It would appear that enterprise is more a reflection of other factors, such as management, than budget or staff size.

Unearned income versus enterprise

Tables B-5 and B-6 compare the percentages of enterprise revenues to that of unearned income, both based on total income. In table B-5, percentages are calculated as a percentage of the *total* sample. For example, 20 percent of the total sample, regardless of the unearned income level, indicated *no* enterprise revenue. In table B-6, percentages are calculated for each unearned income level. Thus, 60 percent of the organizations with 80 percent or more of their income coming from unearned sources have no enterprise revenues.

Table B-5.

UNEARNED INCOME VERSUS ENTERPRISE—TOTAL SAMPLE

UI/TR[a]	Enterprise Revenues as a Percentage of Total Revenue					
	0%	1–1.99%	2–4.99%	5–9.99%	10% or more	*Total*
More than 80%	20	4	4	4	1	33
61–80%	6	3	5	1	6	21
41–60%	6	3	6	3	8	26
26–40%	—	3	3	2	6	14
25% or less	3	—	2	—	1	6
Total	35	13	20	10	22	100

a. *Unearned income as a percentage of total revenue.*

Table B-6.

UNEARNED INCOME VERSUS ENTERPRISE BY UNEARNED
INCOME LEVEL

| | Enterprise Revenues as a Percentage of Total Revenue | | | | | |
UI/TR[a]	0%	1–1.99%	2–4.99%	5–9.99%	10% or more	*Total*
More than 80%	60	14	11.5	11.5	3	100
61–80%	29	14	24	4	29	100
41–60%	22	11	22	11	33	100
26–40%	—	27	20	13	40	100
25% or less	50	—	33	—	17	100

a. *Unearned income as a percentage of total revenue.*

In summary, the data show that—

☐ More than one-third of the sample for which data were available had no enterprise revenues at all.

☐ More than one-third of our sample had 80 percent or more of their total budget generated by unearned income. Of these, 60 percent had no enterprise revenues at all, the remainder of their revenues presumably being made up of fees for service or admissions fees.

☐ Less than 10 percent of the sample had less than one-fourth of their total revenues from unearned sources. Of this small group, one-half had no enterprise activities at all. The other half generated from 2 percent to over 10 percent of their revenues from enterprise.

☐ *Almost one-fourth of the sample had enterprise revenues comprising 10 percent or more of their total revenues.* In general, organizations at the high and low ends of the unearned-to-total-income scale were *least* likely to have significant enterprise revenues. The middle range provides the most data on significant levels of enterprise, once again supporting the contention that enterprise is a function of what is going on in each particular organization rather than any fiscal measure.

Endowments

Our sample was evenly divided between organizations with endowments and those without.

☐ The older the responding organization, the more likely it was to have an endowment.

☐ As table B-7 shows, 85 percent of the respondents 76 years or older have endowments.

☐ There also appears to be a distinct line of demarcation at about 25 years in terms of the likelihood of a nonprofit's having an endowment.

Table B-7.

ENDOWMENT AS FACTOR OF AGE

Age	Percentage of Sample Organizations with Endowments
76 years or older	85
51 to 75 years	60
26 to 50 years	60
16 to 25 years	36
11 to 15 years	10.5
10 years and under	6
Total with endowments	50

Table B-8 shows the distribution of endowments by type of organization. It also shows the average age of our endowed sample and the average age of our total sample. With few exceptions, the data show that older, more established nonprofits are more likely to have endowments. One category, zoos, has a higher overall age than those of endowed zoos, which can be explained by the fact that several responding zoological parks are run by states or municipalities. This funding situation has made endowments unnecessary. With the exception of symphony orchestras, all performing arts organizations fell at the newer and less-endowed end. The fact that our sample shows the average age of all orchestras as being higher than those with endowments is a peculiarity of our responding sample. According to the American Symphony Orchestra League, almost all of their members have endowments of some sort. It is also worth noting that our questionnaire did not ask for the nonprofit to distinguish, as presented in the American Institute of Certified Public Accountants' Statement of Position 78-10, "Accounting Principles and Reporting Practices for Certain Non-Profit Organizations," between true endowments (i.e., "restricted") and unrestricted funds, which are not to be regarded as true endowments. As a result, there may be some inconsistency in the responses.

Table B-8.

ORGANIZATION TYPES, RANKED BY PERCENTAGE WITH
ENDOWMENTS

	Percentage with Endowments	Average Age of Endowed Organizations (years)	Average Age of Samples (years)
Colleges/ universities	100	145	145
Child welfare	85	98.5	97
Camps	80	85	68
Private schools	75	169	146
Orchestras	60	30	34
Museums	56	63	44
Family services	56	75	68
Historical societies	45	43	39
Handicapped	25	48	26
Theaters	20	37.5	16
Zoos	16	17	33
Dance/ballet	0	21.5	21.5
Media arts	0	9	9
Opera	0	19	19

We have already seen that the endowed organizations tend to be older than the unendowed. Beyond that, an analysis of these charts reveals very little except to reinforce previous statements that the pursuit of enterprise seems to be independent of age, size, or endowment.

☐ Over 60 percent of both endowed and unendowed organizations receive less than 5 percent of their revenues from enterprise.

☐ A higher percentage of unendowed organizations have no enterprise revenues (37 versus 27 percent).

☐ A higher percentage of endowed organizations earn 10 percent or more of their income from enterprise (20 versus 14.5 percent).

When Enterprises Were Started

Table B-9 shows the distribution of the respondents' enterprises in terms of when the enterprises were started.

Table B-9.

WHEN ENTERPRISES WERE STARTED

Years	Percentage of Sample
Before 1940	9
1940–1949	2
1950–1959	8
1960–1969	12
1970-present	69
	100

Our sample indicates that well over two-thirds of the enterprises started in the 1970s. The earliest enterprises tended to be retail stores, publishing ventures, restaurants, and educational activities (e.g., lectures, "how-to courses," etc.) The post-1970s enterprises are of various types.

Appendix C

SAMPLE COMPARISON

Because of the small size of our sample, we decided to test the conclusions we drew against the wider universe of nonprofits. To do this we secured data from a number of professional organizations that compile statistics on their members. The statistics came in a variety of forms and at varying levels of depth. Few organizations provide in-depth information on "enterprise income" per se. However, in most cases it was possible to arrive at an estimate for "earned income as a percentage of total income." In a few cases we could use our own definition of enterprise to determine an *estimate* of "enterprise income as a percentage of total income."

If the information was not available, it is indicated in the table as "NA." This was sometimes true for our own sample as well. For some categories in our study, no data were collected. In some cases, information did not seem to be available; in others, our own sample was insufficient to warrant comparison.

Table C-1 compares our data sample to the overall category data, as provided by the source listed, or as extrapolated from information supplied by sources for the following:

☐ Average income
☐ Average earned income/average income
☐ Average enterprise income/average income

For each category in the chart, a commentary that provides additional supporting data or explanatory material follows. Overall, we believe our data sample fairly represents the larger universe.

Commentary to Table C-1

Blind

☐ Of the source sample of 147 agencies, no income figures were available for 26.
☐ 40 percent of the sample indicate "workshop" as a source of income.
☐ 78 percent have fee/subcontract and/or workshop revenues, but specific amounts generated were not provided.
☐ Our sample, based on questionnaire responses, was too small to warrant comparison.

Child Welfare

☐ As for family services, it is not clear from the data provided if there are any enterprise revenues.
☐ "Earned" or fee income provides 9.5 percent of income.
☐ In addition, 46 percent of income is other fees—"payments for service on case-by-case basis" from governmental source.

Dance

☐ Earned income as a percentage of total income has grown from 38 to 54 percent from 1975 to 1980.
☐ Our sample was small and heavily represented by the larger regional companies.
☐ The National Association for Regional Ballet is completing a full study.

Family Services

☐ Earned income is definitely on the rise.
☐ 99 percent of sample have income from "casework counseling fees" (compared with 89 percent in 1960).
☐ 64 percent of sample have "other client fees."
☐ In 1980, 42 percent of the source sample received 10 percent or more of their income from "casework counseling fees" (compared with 12 percent in 1960).
☐ The smaller the agency, the higher the percentage of total income earned from fees.
☐ From the information provided, it was not clear that there was any enterprise income. Our own sample showed very little enterprise,

although one agency's enterprises accounted for 50 percent of its total income, primarily from rentals.

Media Arts

☐ The National Alliance of Media Arts Centers conducted a survey completed in 1982. The information used was provided by Robert Haller, NAMAC chairman, in the August 1981 issue of *Media Arts*.
☐ Government funding equaled 30 percent of total income.
☐ Media arts centers earn income through

- Film screenings
- Broadcast programming
- Film and video equipment rentals
- Education/lectures
- Books/publications

☐ Specific amounts were not provided.

Museums

☐ Of the survey of 4,409 museums, 50 percent are history; 18 percent, science; 14 percent, art; 9 percent, general; 4 percent, specialized; 1 percent, children's.
☐ 53 percent of museums are nonprofit; 33 percent, governmental.
☐ 53 percent of museums "broke even"; 36 percent had a net gain; 11 percent had a net loss.
☐ The mean staff size of museums experiencing a net loss was approximately *twice* that of those experiencing a net gain.
☐ 42 percent of museum operating income was *earned*.
☐ Specialized museums *earned* 61 percent of income.
☐ 54.2 percent of museums have income-producing bookstores.
☐ 14.2 percent of museums have income-producing conference facilities.
☐ 12 percent of museums have an income-producing restaurant.
☐ 8.6 percent of museums have income-producing "other facilities."
☐ 37 percent of museums have a cash-operating income of from $1,000 to $25,000.
☐ 15 percent of museums have a cash-operating income of $25,001 to $50,000.
☐ 11 percent have a cash-operating income of more than $400,000.
☐ 32 percent charge general admissions fees (61.5 percent of specialized, 40 percent of children's, 38.8 percent of science, 24.8 percent of general museums, 15.9 percent of art).
☐ Of the 32 percent charging general admission fees, 88 percent have a fixed charge; 12 percent, a suggested charge.
☐ 58 percent of museums with incomes of more than $400,000 charge admission.

- ☐ 72.8 percent have *no* endowment funds.
- ☐ 78 percent have a board of trustees.

Opera

- ☐ Sample of 109 is for opera companies with budgets of more than $100,000 only and excludes the Metropolitan Opera.
- ☐ 68 additional companies had costs during the 1979-80 season of $3.7 million, an average of $54,000.
- ☐ 20 of the larger companies had not yet covered costs as of the study date (November 1980).
- ☐ 60 percent of the 109 companies showed a decrease of income for box office and flat performance fees averaging 37.8 percent.
- ☐ Sample of data on a variety of companies shows:
  - Budget range of $540,000 to $2.8 million.
  - Range of earned income (box office plus performance fees plus other earned income) 31 to 63 percent.

Private Secondary Schools

- ☐ No total figures were provided, so they were extrapolated from figures on a "per student" basis.
- ☐ Our sample was small and respondents were (in all but one case) the largest, best-endowed schools.
- ☐ Categories included are day and secondary boarding schools.

Symphonies

- ☐ Overall, orchestras show a deficit of 2.3 percent.
- ☐ Over the past decade, earned income as a percentage of gross income has gone up 2 percent (to 48 percent) and contributed income as a share of gross income has gone down 3 percent (to 29 percent).
- ☐ The breakdown of types of orchestras is as follows:

Major (over $2 million)	32
Regional ($500,000 to $2 million)	34
Metro ($100,000 to $500,000)	115
Urban ($50,000 to $100,000)	85
Community (under $50,000)	926
College	385
Total	**1,577**

- ☐ In our sample, only one orchestra was not a major or regional orchestra.

Theater

☐ 54 percent of Theatre Communications Group's sample had a deficit in 1981 (compared with 43 percent in 1980).

☐ From "Theatre Facts '81" (emphasis added):

- "Despite increased attendance and productivity, *ticket income declined* in relation to meeting total expenses."
- "Much of the *earned income gain was derived from secondary activities, including concessions, booked-in events and interest.*"
- Overall, earnings increased by nearly 30 percent, while contributed income from all sources increased at a rate just 3.2 percent ahead of inflation."
- "As theatres were required to generate more income from secondary activities and to solicit thousands of new donors, the *administrative labor force was increased by nearly 20 percent.*"
- "The financial trends continue to indicate a measure of stability through adaptation to changing circumstances; however, the economic support structure is *seen not to be conducive to new advances in artistic areas.*"

☐ Over the past five years,

- Concessions experienced a 30 percent growth rate.
- Programs advertising experienced a 69 percent growth rate.
- Booked-in events experienced a 28 percent growth rate.

☐ Nonticket earnings were 22 percent of expenses in 1981 (compared with 17 percent of expenses in 1977).

☐ Royalty income (the "Broadway Transfer"):

	1980	1979	1978	1977
Number of respondents	12	12	10	8
Average royalty income per respondent ($)	11,539	7,803	11,755	8,264

These statistics dispel the myth that the "Broadway Transfer," except in a very small number of cases (e.g., "A Chorus Line" and "Ain't Misbehavin' "), does provide significant revenue streams.

Zoos/Aquariums

☐ Statistics on earned revenues were not provided.

☐ However, 31 percent of the sample of 126 zoos list "earned revenues" as a source of income.

☐ Of the source sample, 90 are municipal zoos; 19, societies; 7, county; 5, state; 2, federal; and 3, miscellaneous.

☐ Our sample was one-half municipal, one-fourth society, and one-fourth state.

Table C-1.
OUTSIDE SOURCE SAMPLES,
COMPARED TO STUDY SAMPLES

Category	Source of Data and Number in Sample	Average Income ($000)		Average Percentage Earned Income		Average Percentage Enterprise	
		Category Data	Study Sample	Category Data	Study Sample	Category Data	Study Sample
Blind	American Fndn. for the Blind (121)	1,400	NA	NA	NA	[a]	NA
Child Welfare	Child Welfare League of America (204)	1,450	2,100	9.5	15	NA	Under 1
Colleges/universities[b]	—	—	NA	—	52	—	3-23[c]
Dance	Nat'l. Assn. for Regional Ballet (91)	75	627	54	50	NA	1
Family services	Family Service Assn. of America (247)	390	467	13	22	Under 1	0-53[c]
Handicapped[b]	—	—	930	NA	13	NA	2
Media arts	Nat'l. Alliance of Media Arts Ctrs. (64)	117	233	46	42	NA	10
Museums	Nat'l. Center for Educational Statistics (4,409)	250	1,180	42	31	12	11
Opera	Opera News (109) [Central Opera Service Questionnaire]	1,225	775	48	46	NA	2
Private secondary schools	National Association of Independent Schools (208)	1,766	9,690	69-89[c]	70	4-10[c]	3
Symphonies	Amer. Symphony Orchestra League Regional (32) Major (32)	6,573 1,324	2,286[d]	55 56	51[d]	15 13	NA
Theater	Theatre Communications Group (121)	917	1,225	71	59	11	5
Zoos/aquariums	Amer. Assn. of Zoological Parks and Aquariums (126)	1,220	1,870	NA	47	NA	18

[a]Approximately 40 percent have workshop sales and subcontracting revenues.
[b]See "Commentary" for further explanations.
[c]The sample size was quite small and the range varied greatly; an average percentage is not meaningful.
[d]Symphony data were provided for two size ranges; the study sample combines both categories.